ILTS 155 Learning Behavior Specialist I

Illinois Licensure Testing System

By: Preparing Teachers In America™

This page is intentionally left blank.

This publication is not an affiliation, or sponsorship, of Pearson Education or the National Evaluation Series.

© 2016 by Preparing Teachers In America

Publication by Preparing Teachers In America Publication Services, a division of Preparing Teachers In America

All rights reserved. The text of this publication, or any part thereof, may not be reproduced in any manner whatsoever without the written permission from Preparing Teachers In America. Any violation of copyright laws will be subject to possible criminal charges and/or civil penalties.

Printed in the United States of America

ISBN-13 978-1539500216

ISBN-10: 1539500217

The author and the publisher make no warranties with respect to the correctness or completeness of the content contain in this publication and specifically disclaim all warranties whatsoever. Advice, strategies, and suggestions described may not be suitable for every case. Providing web addresses or other (information) services in this publication does not mean/imply that the author or publisher endorses information or websites. Neither the author nor publisher shall be liable for damages arising herefrom. Websites may be infected by computer viruses. The author and publisher shall not be held responsible for any damage resulted herefrom. Websites (content) may have altered since the time the author described them in this booklet and this booklet is read. There are no guarantees attached to the publication. The content of this publication is best practices, suggestions, common mistakes, and interpretation, and the author and the publisher are not responsible for any information contained in the publication.

Any services provided by the publication, authors, or company are with the understanding that services can be terminated with or without notice. In rendering services, the author and the publisher are not responsible for any information communicated. Users agree not to hold the service (author/publisher/company) or its employees liable for any services (information) provided or any information displayed on the website. Users release the service from any claims or any kind of damage. The author, publisher, services, and/or company are not responsible for any accuracy or legitimacy of the information provided during rendering services. There are no guarantees attached to services.

No institutions (public or private) have permission to reproduce (in any form) the contents of this publication.

This page is intentionally left blank.

Free Online Email Tutoring Services

All preparation guides purchased directly from Preparing Teachers In America includes a free three month email tutoring subscription. Any resale of preparation guides does not qualify for a free email tutoring subscription.

What is Email Tutoring?

Email Tutoring allows buyers to send questions to tutors via email. Buyers can send any questions regarding the exam processes, strategies, content questions, or practice questions.

Preparing Teachers In America reserves the right not to answer questions with or without reason(s).

How to use Email Tutoring?

Buyers need to send an email to onlinepreparationservices@gmail.com requesting email tutoring services. Buyers may be required to confirm the email address used to purchase the preparation guide or additional information prior to using email tutoring. Once email tutoring subscription is confirmed, buyers will be provided an email address to send questions to. The three month period will start the day the subscription is confirmed.

Any misuse of email tutoring services will result in termination of service. Preparing Teachers In America reserves the right to terminate email tutoring subscription at anytime with or without notice.

Comments and Suggestions

All comments and suggestions for improvements for the study guide and email tutoring services need to be sent to onlinepreparationservices@gmail.com.

This page is intentionally left blank.

Table of Content

About the Exam and Study Guide 1

Exam Answer Sheet 5

Practice Exam Questions 7

Practice Exam - Correct Answer Sheet 51

Practice Exam Questions and Answers 53

This page is intentionally left blank.

About the Exam and Study Guide

What is the ILST Learning Behavior Specialist I (155) Exam?

The ILST Learning Behavior Specialist I is an exam to measure potential teachers' competencies related to special education instructions and assessments for all grade levels. The test measures if individuals have the knowledge necessary to start teaching special education students. The exam is based largely on teacher preparation standards, and the following are content areas covered by the special education exam:
- Students with Disabilities
- Assessment and Program Planning
- Learning Environments
- Instructional Practices
- Foundations and Professional Practice

The exam is timed at 225 minutes and consists of 125 questions. The 150 selected-response questions are based on knowledge obtained in a bachelor's degree program. The exam contains some questions that may not count toward the score.

What topics are covered on the exam?

The following are some topics covered on the exam:

- characteristics of students with disabilities
- factors that affect development and learning in students with disabilities
- types of formal and informal assessments
- effective instructional practices
- strategies for developing students' communication and social skills
- effective behavioral interventions for students with disabilities
- strategies for teaching functional living skills
- promoting successful transitions for students with disabilities
- the historical, legal, and ethical foundations of special education.
- the professional roles and responsibilities of the special education teacher

What is included in this study guide book?

This guide includes one full length practice exam for the ILST Learning Behavior Specialist I along with detail explanations. The recommendation is to take the exam under exam conditions and a quiet environment.

This page is intentionally left blank.

Practice Test 1

This page is intentionally left blank.

Exam Answer Sheet

Below is an optional answer sheet to use to document answers.

Question Number	Selected Answer	Question Number	Selected Answer	Question Number	Selected Answer	Question Number	Selected Answer	Question Number	Selected Answer
1		31		61		91		121	
2		32		62		92		122	
3		33		63		93		123	
4		34		64		94		124	
5		35		65		95		125	
6		36		66		96			
7		37		67		97			
8		38		68		98			
9		39		69		99			
10		40		70		100			
11		41		71		101			
12		42		72		102			
13		43		73		103			
14		44		74		104			
15		45		75		105			
16		46		76		106			
17		47		77		107			
18		48		78		108			
19		49		79		109			
20		50		80		110			
21		51		81		111			
22		52		82		112			
23		53		83		113			
24		54		84		114			
25		55		85		115			
26		56		86		116			
27		57		87		117			
28		58		88		118			
29		59		89		119			
30		60		90		120			

This page is intentionally left blank.

Practice Exam Questions

QUESTION 1

Which of the following type of equipment would be best for a student with cerebral palsy to eat?

A. swivel spoon
B. small spoon
C. fork
D. right-angle spoon

Answer:

QUESTION 2

How many days can a special education student be suspended?

A. 3 days
B. 5 days
C. 10 days
D. 15 days

Answer:

QUESTION 3

Jake is an eleventh grade student with a specific learning disability. He informs his special education teacher that he desires a career related to gardening. Which of the following is the best first step for the teacher to take to support the student's long term goal?

A. provide brochures related to colleges and careers focusing on gardening
B. have the student complete an interest inventory to define objectives in detail
C. inform student to pursue education in agriculture
D. help the student find a summer internship related to gardening

Answer:

QUESTION 4

A parent made a request to do assessments for his child as the parent is concerned that his son might have ADHD. Which of the following procedures will likely increase accuracy in the results of the assessment?

    A. have two special education teachers administer the same assessment and compare results
    B. schedule several short testing sessions instead of one long session
    C. include hands on activities to engage the student
    D. inform the student a reward will be given at the completion of the assessment

Answer:

QUESTION 5

    I. phonology
    II. morphology
    III. semantics
    IV. syntax
    V. pragmatics

Which of the following correctly orders the levels of language?

    A. I, II, III, IV, V
    B. I, II, IV, III, V
    C. V, IV, III, II, I
    D. I, III, II, V, IV

Answer:

QUESTION 6

Which of the following ages are the best to introduce effective play?

    A. 0 to 1
    B. 1 to 3
    C. 3 to 4
    D. 4 to 5

Answer:

QUESTION 7

Which of the following is NOT a written expression?

- A. vocabulary
- B. morphology
- C. content
- D. sentence structure

Answer:

QUESTION 8

Which of the following is NOT an example of low tech assistance device?

- A. pencil grip
- B. splint
- C. paper stabilizer
- D. voice synthesizers

Answer:

QUESTION 9

A student with a stuttering problem has a communication disorder with which of the following?

- A. blending
- B. fluency
- C. articulation
- D. dialect

Answer:

QUESTION 10

Which of the following is the best to use for a student with difficulty listening when communicating instructions?

- A. visual stimulant
- B. short and clear directions
- C. questions and answer approach
- D. positive reinforcement and role playing

Answer:

QUESTION 11

What does the Council for Exceptional Children focus on?

   A. provide professional development for special education teachers
   B. support in the development of standards
   C. advance the success of children with exceptionalities
   D. all of the above

Answer:

QUESTION 12

Impairments in social perceptions, interaction, and nonverbal communication with no major cognitive delays are characterized by _____.

   A. ADHD
   B. Asperger syndrome
   C. Williams syndrome
   D. Down syndrome

Answer:

QUESTION 13

A special education student has multiple disabilities, which include emotional disturbance and cognitive impairment. The student is in a general education classroom with a 1:1 special education consultant. The sitting is not enough to support the student. Which of the following is the next best level of support to provide the student?

   A. full time
   B. itinerant
   C. instruction afterschool
   D. alterative

Answer:

QUESTION 14

A special education teacher uses various methods, strategies, resources, and technology to support diverse learners targeting strengths and weaknesses. Which of the following practices is the special education teacher implementing?

A. technology-based learning
B. direct instruction
C. differentiated instruction
D. targeted instruction

Answer:

QUESTION 15

A fifth-grade student with a specific learning disability functions at a third-grade level in written expression. The student communicates when asked a question during class discussion, but he is unable to put ideas in writing. Which of the following is the best approach to facilitate the understanding of the student's learning when given a curriculum-based science test that includes writing an essay?

A. allow the student to complete the test with oral responses
B. give the student extra time to complete assignment
C. help the student start off the essay
D. give the student a multiple choice assignment

Answer:

QUESTION 16

Mr. Martin has a 12th-grade student with Oppositional defiant disorder (ODD), and the student's has the most difficulty in reacting to stressful situation and gets extremely negative. Which of the following is the best first treatment approach to take with this student?

A. Parent-Management Training Programs
B. Cognitive Problem-Solving Skills Training
C. Social Skills Programs
D. Medication

Answer:

QUESTION 17

James is a student with severe, multiple disabilities. Which of the following strategies is best to effectively elicit an orienting response from James?

    A. give partial answers to reach full answers
    B. use modeling to give examples
    C. slightly change familiar activities
    D. provide reward for reaching correct answers

Answer:

QUESTION 18

Kevin is a ninth-grade student who is highly distractible individual with a learning disability. Which of the following is the best first step to take in developing a behavior management plan?

    A. determine if there is a connection with distractibility and learning disability
    B. determine factors that contribute to effective behavior
    C. define attending behaviors in operational terms to achieve
    D. review any previous behavior management plan

Answer:

QUESTION 19

Which of the following is the best instructional strategy for assisting students with fine-motor impairments to master the skills needed to dress?

    A. provide repeated opportunities to observe
    B. give repeated opportunities to apply the skills
    C. give opportunities to dress and undress dolls
    D. provide repeated opportunities to identify clothing

Answer:

QUESTION 20

A ninth-grade special education teacher is seeking to support a student who is:

- new to the United States
- English language learner
- diagnosed with orthopedic impairment
- meeting classroom expectations
- reluctant to response to oral questions from teacher questions
- willingly interacts with students during learning activities
- unwilling to interact with the teacher

Which of the following is the first question to answer to support the student's learning?

A. Is the student's disability impacting his development of English skills?
B. Is the student placed in the right grade level?
C. Is he accustomed to different teaching practices from his home country?
D. Does he have an IEP?

Answer:

QUESTION 21

A 10th-grade student with an intellectual disability is enrolled in a school-based training program to developing job skills. The student is first required to do an activity measuring speed and accuracy of sorting. Which of the following best describes the activity?

A. criterion-referenced test
B. norm-referenced test
C. performance-based assessment
D. scaled assessment

Answer:

QUESTION 22

Compared to peers without disability, a 17-year-old student with a mild intellectual disability is likely to have more struggles with which of the following tasks?

    A. greeting individuals arriving at open house
    B. communicating with peers during lunch
    C. completing three-step task for science experiment
    D. recalling a set of steps to complete a science experiment informed by the teacher a few minutes earlier

Answer:

QUESTION 23

A special education teacher is planning to teach a seventh-grade student with autism to brush his teeth and comb his hair. Which of the following instructional methods is most effective for teaching these skills?

    A. sequencing chaining
    B. backward chaining
    C. peer modeling
    D. forward chaining

Answer:

QUESTION 24

Which of the following is the best approach for an inexperienced special education teacher to learn about instructional practice?

    A. use a website that ends with .gov or .org
    B. ask a general education teacher
    C. use college textbook
    D. an educational blog

Answer:

QUESTION 25

A tenth-grade student is defiant, spiteful, and negative. The student is showing signs of
_____.

    A. ADHS
    B. ODD
    C. ADD
    D. OCD

Answer:

QUESTION 26

A tenth-grade student with a mild intellectual disability and dyscalculia is getting instruction in daily living skills. Of the following tasks, which is likely the most difficult for this student?

    A. counting up to five
    B. recognizing common objects
    C. applying previous knowledge to different environment
    D. identifying time

Answer:

QUESTION 27

A prescribed stimulant medication for ADHD includes common side effects of
_____.

    A. poor circulation
    B. inability to concentrate
    C. loss of appetite
    D. low blood pressure

Answer:

QUESTION 28

Parents of a secondary student are meeting with the special education teacher. Which of the following strategies will foster effective communication during the conference?

    A. use direct language without technical terms
    B. engage in discussion related to activities done during the weekend
    C. ask parents to write questions before coming to the meeting
    D. have research articles on topics of concern that might surface

Answer:

QUESTION 29

A special education teacher has four students in a group, and two of the students have specific learning disabilities. The teacher is having difficulty getting one student with learning disability to learn adding fractions. Which of the following is the best approach to get the students to learn adding fraction?

    A. additional practice
    B. one-on-one instruction
    C. use blocks
    D. use alternative method

Answer:

QUESTION 30

Which of the following math skills is most likely the easiest for a student with autism to acquire?

    A. adding numbers
    B. subtracting numbers
    C. reciting numbers in order
    D. writing numbers

Answer:

QUESTION 31

Why is math so difficult to learn for individuals at early age with ADHD?

A. includes numbers
B. includes multistep procedures
C. takes time to complete problems
D. requires memory, problem solving and organizing skills

Answer:

QUESTION 32

Mr. Sheppard, a fifth-grade special education science teacher, is working with autistic students to spot simple machines in daily surroundings. Which of the following daily objects would be the best example of a lever?

A. a ramp
B. skateboard
C. hammer
D. desk

Answer:

QUESTION 33

Carla is the mother of Susan, who attends secondary education school. Susan has come home multiple times with scratches inflicted by another student, Martha. Which of the following best indicates the most inappropriate response for the teacher to undertake along with what action the teacher should undertake?

A. The teacher would be wrong to tell the parent that Martha and Susan had difficulty working together that day. The teacher would be right in informing the parent that she will monitor both students closely going forward and report back.
B. The teacher would be wrong to generalize that there might have been some provocative verbal communication, which resulted in the scratches. The teacher would be right to take action by involving the principal and recommending appropriate punishments.
C. The teacher would be wrong to suggest that Martha's action resulted due to issues occurring in her family. The teacher would be right in informing the parent that she will monitor both students closely going forward and report back.
D. The teacher would be wrong to generalize that there might have been some provocative verbal communication, which resulted in the scratches. The teacher would be right in informing the parent that she will monitor both students closely going forward and report back.

Answer:

QUESTION 34

Mary, an eighth grade special education teacher, is alarmed by one student's appearance and behavior as the perceptions seems that she has been physically abused at home. According to state and federal law, the teacher is required to immediately:

A. inform the school nurse to allow him or her to take appropriate action
B. ensure her suspicions are reported in compliance with state/federal law and requirements
C. contact the parents to inform them of the situation
D. ask indirect questions to confirm suspicions and proceed in contacting law enforcement

Answer:

QUESTION 35

    I. all special education students in America
    II. students with severe disabilities
    III. students eligible for special education in public schools

IEP is/are required for:

A. I only
B. I and II
C. II and III
D. I, II, and III

Answer:

QUESTION 36

A first-grade teacher designed an activity using balls for her six students with specific learning disabilities. The teacher marks off a space and provides balls of different sizes, materials, and color. Pairs of students are allowed 30 minutes to explore the balls and 15 minutes to discuss the question, "How did the balls roll?" Which of the following type of teaching is being implemented in this activity?

A. circular instruction
B. inquiry instruction
C. direct instruction
D. indirect instruction

Answer:

QUESTION 37

Fourth-grade students with learning disabilities have been identifying planets in the solar system and their position in relation to the Sun. Which of the following culminating activities would be the best for assessment purposes of the students' learning?

    A. students complete a final assessment on the unit topic
    B. students complete a exit-slip on the unit topic
    C. students complete a report on the unit topic
    D. students complete a science fair project on the unit topic

Answer:

QUESTION 38

A special education math teacher has a student with IEP to complete classroom assignments independently 85% of the time. The special education teacher is modeling and doing group activities to teach and engage the student. Which of the following methods is the best to help the student work with increasing independence?

    A. fading
    B. independence
    C. ignoring
    D. self-grading

Answer:

QUESTION 39

A special education teacher works with several eighth-grade students with specific learning disabilities in reading. In addition, these students do not have the desire to read for pleasure. Which of the following methods is best to foster students' interest in independent reading?

    A. establish a reading program that rewards students
    B. provide students with reading material tailored to their reading abilities
    C. give students more opportunity to spend time in library
    D. establish a goal for the class to reach in regards to reading books

Answer:

QUESTION 40

- delay in counting
- difficulty in memorizing arithmetic facts
- delay in addition

The above are most likely associated with which of the following disability?

A. dyscalculia
B. acalculia
C. dyslipidemia
D. dyscalculia

Answer:

QUESTION 41

A teacher plans to inform the parents of their child's results on an evaluation. The child is a fifth-grade student with ADD. To ensure the information is effectively communicated, the teacher should:

A. develop a chart summarizing the results
B. use non-technical language that the parents will understand
C. provide background information on the assessment
D. show parents worksheets completed by the student

Answer:

QUETSION 42

A special education teacher has a student with epilepsy. If the student has a seizure in class, the teacher should first:

A. call for the school nurse to help
B. move the other students to another room
C. remove objects located around the student
D. gently restrain the student

Answer:

QUESTION 43

What is typical way for a pre-kindergarten autistic child to communicate with a teacher?

- A. verbal
- B. non-verbal
- C. written
- D. communication board

Answer:

QUESTION 44

James is a tenth-grade student with a Functional Behavioral Assessment (FBA). He has unexpectedly become physically aggressive with others in school. To ensure effective intervention, which of the following should be done first by the IEP team?

- A. interview peers and teachers
- B. define behavior in measureable terms
- C. predict reasoning for changes in behavior
- D. develop a plan to collect data

Answer:

QUESTION 45

- I. handles a book properly
- II. awareness that reading is done from left to right
- III. awareness that words are put together to convey information

The above are signs that demonstrate a child is developing skills associated with:

- A. phonics
- B. fluency
- C. concept of print
- D. ability to read

Answer:

QUESTION 46

A special education teacher moves his finger continuously along each line of the text as he reads a Big Book. This approach is most useful for supporting students' understanding the concept that:

A. print can be big and small
B. print has directionality
C. sentence consist of words
D. words are decodable

Answer:

QUESTION 47

I. Diagnostic assessment allow teachers to map out a route, using existing knowledge to build upon.
II. Response to Intervention is an approach for the early identification and support of students with learning and behavior needs.
III. Screening assessments are used to determine whether students are ready to end a course.

Of the above, which of the following is/are correctly stated?

A. I only
B. II only
C. I and II
D. I, II, and III

Answer:

QUESTION 48

Which of the following assessment is used to evaluate student learning at the conclusion of an instructional period (ex. at the end of a unit)?

A. formative assessment
B. interim assessment
C. summative assessment
D. placement assessment

Answer:

QUESTION 49

A teacher is promoting the idea of introducing fundamental structure of all subject areas in the early years of individual's education and revisiting them in more complex forms over time. This idea is called:

A. complex curriculum
B. spiral curriculum
C. reciprocal curriculum
D. instructional curriculum

Answer:

QUESTION 50

    I.   summary of the student's process in vocational skills
    II.   summary of the present level of development
    III.   statement of major expected outcomes

Which of the following is/are included in an Individual Family Service Plan?

A. I only
B. I and II
C. II and III
D. I, II, and III

Answer:

QUESTION 51

A special education teacher is displaying equipment to show various types of objects found in a lab. One student starts playing with one of the equipment. What is the best type of social discipline action to be taken?

A. remove the student from the classroom and explain to other students this behavior is unacceptable
B. use the equipment student has next in explaining the equipment of the lab
C. place the student away from the equipment
D. move closer to the student to let him know the instructor is aware of the behavior

Answer:

QUESTION 52

Which of the following activities would be the most meaningful science experience for first grade students with mild learning disabilities?

A. participating in hands-on instruction from a textbook
B. engaging in self-generated, open-ended investigations
C. viewing an educational video with the class
D. conducting an experiment in lab

Answer:

QUESTION 53

Mr. Mark, a special education teacher, has a student that has been diagnosed with a disease, and the student will be missing school frequently. The student is in the process of being tested to confirm the prognosis. In class, Mr. Mark's best action to take is:

A. to observe the student carefully and ask the student frequently if she is doing well
B. to inform the student that she can go to the nurse at anytime with permission
C. to send reports to the parents on how the student is doing during class
D. to assist her in understanding the disease and let her know she has the support of her teacher

Answer:

QUESTION 54

Blake is a new student from another state, and he has separation anxiety. At the beginning of class during circle time, he does not want to let his father go. The best action for the teacher is to:

A. have the father come visit Blake a couple of times per day
B. have the father remain with Blake for 15 minutes and, then, ask him to leave
C. have the father participate in circle time, and when Blake is involved, have the parent sneak out of the room
D. introduce Blake to two friends and ask him to sit between them and engage in a discussion

Answer:

QUESTION 55

A special education preschool teacher, Mrs. Martin, plays a game with her students in which she says a familiar word and her students respond by repeating and drawing out each individual sound. For example, when Mrs. Martin says the word "kiss", the students will say "kkkkiiiissss." This activity is an oral language activity that involves phonemic segmentation. This activity most likely supports which of the following future literacy skills?

A. writing letters
B. spelling
C. recognizing
D. word definitions

Answer:

QUESTION 56

I. carries toys or objects while walking
II. kicks a ball forward
III. jumps in place
IV. throws a ball overhand with some accuracy

Of the above gross motor skills, which of the following are characterized as actions taken by a typical 18 to 36 month old child?

A. I and II
B. I and III
C. I and IV
D. II and IV

Answer:

QUESTION 57

During a parent teacher conference, a seventh-grade special education teacher informs the parents of a student that their child likely has ADHD. What did the teacher do wrong?

A. The teacher did nothing wrong.
B. The teacher did not administer an informal assessment to determine if the student had ADHD.
C. The teacher did not use an appropriate individual to test, confirm, and diagnose the student.
D. The teacher informed the parents of a "likely" scenario.

Answer:

QUESTION 58

Of the following, early childhood students typically develop which expressive language skills last?

A. use of four words to make a short sentence
B. use of few words to make a request
C. use of pronouns to indicate people
D. use of conjugations to link simple ideas

Answer:

QUESTION 59

Family Educational Rights and Privacy Action (FERPA) protect students' records at school institutions in America. Which of the following situations of a request to see a student's records will be approved?

A. A parent seeking to confirm a student's enrollment in the appropriate special education program.
B. A parent seeking to confirm a student's IEP is acceptable to ensure proper learning.
C. A parent questioning a student's placement for special education classes for the new school year.
D. A parent questioning a student's grades and requesting to see all assignment grades.

Answer:

QUESTION 60

Mr. Jon has been informed that a new student will be coming into his class. The student has special needs. Mr. Jon conducts a meeting with the special education instructor to review the goals in the new student's IEP. Which of the following describe Mr. Jon's responsibilities regarding the IEP goals?

A. ensuring that the goals are kept confidential
B. setting up an incentive approach to ensure goals are being accomplished
C. having activities in the classroom related to the IEP goals
D. selecting the most critical goals for planning lesson plans

Answer:

QUESTION 61

A second grade teacher notices a child removing food from lunch and hiding it in his backpack. The teacher notices this behavior and discusses it with the student after class. In the discussion, the student mentions his father lost his job and that there is not much food to eat. Which of the following is the most appropriate first response for the teacher to take?

A. contact the principal to develop a plan to ensure proper food is given to the student outside of the school
B. contact Child Protective Services (CPS) to report possible neglect at home
C. provide the student with food and snacks to take home going forward
D. speak to the family about relevant community services and support during this difficult time

Answer:

QUESTION 62

Jake is a third grade student who has been diagnosed with a learning disability known as written expression. Of the following, which one is the least restrictive environment?

A. an inclusion classroom
B. a quite environment
C. a separate-closed room
D. a pull-out resource room

Answer:

QUESTION 63

Mrs. Perez teaches fourth grade students. There are 21 students, and three of the students have developmental delays. Which of the following provides Mrs. Perez with the necessary data to differentiate instruction for those three students?

A. discuss with co-teachers on previous methods used in the school
B. monitor students' progress to see what approaches are working
C. ask the students what approach has worked in the past
D. review previous performance records to understand strengths and weaknesses

Answer:

QUESTION 64

Which of the following hand to eye coordination games best fits three to four year olds in a classroom?

A. hide and seek
B. put a circle on board and ask students to throw a rubber ball inside the circle
C. have someone throw a ball and have another child hit the ball with a bat
D. build a structure with blocks

Answer:

QUESTION 65

I. a portfolio
II. an intelligence test
III. an adaptive behavior scale

Of the above, which of the following is/are formal assessment(s)?

A. I and II
B. I and III
C. II and III
D. I, II, and III

Answer:

QUESTION 66

I. a chromosomal disorder
II. mother exposed to lead during pregnancy
III. vaccination

Of the above, which is/are direct cause(s) of Down syndrome?

A. I only
B. II only
C. III only
D. I and II

Answer:

QUESTION 67

Of the following fine motor skills, which of the following does not characterize a 36 to 60 month old child?

A. copies shapes and geometric shapes
B. eats with utensils
C. open doors, with assistance, by turning and pulling doorknobs
D. manipulates small objects with ease

Answer:

QUESTION 68

Which of the following is the best learning objective for a special education class of third-grade learning about money?

A. Students will be able to determine the value of fake money given to them.
B. Students will be able to solve word problems asking them to solve for change left over.
C. Students will be able to represent the value of money in fraction of a dollar.
D. Students will be able to solve problems involving decimal operations.

Answer:

QUESTION 69

A fourth grade teacher notices that her students are having difficulty doing math problems involving fractions. What is the best first step for the teacher to undertake to support the students?

A. have the students complete an assessment on basics of fractions
B. assign the students extra practice on fractions for homework
C. ask the students exactly what there are having difficulty with
D. use direct teaching methods to show how to solve problems with fractions

Answer:

QUESTION 70

At the end of the unit on fraction, Mr. Locke, a special education math teacher, is seeking to determine what the students have learned. Which of the following assessments is the best to implement?

A. authentic assessment
B. standards-based assessment
C. summative assessment
D. norm-referenced assessment

Answer:

QUESTION 71

A child is coming into the classroom next year that is legally blind. What should the teacher request before the upcoming school year?

A. manipulative
B. communication board
C. speakers
D. smart board

Answer:

QUESTION 72

A special diet can be used to prevent learning disabilities in infants who are born with which of the following conditions?

- A. phenylketonuria
- B. down syndrome
- C. fetal alcohol syndrome
- D. none of the above

Answer:

QUESTION 73

Mr. Derrick is a second-grade teacher. He is worried that one of his students, Bill, is having trouble acquiring basic reading skills. Bill has shown the following difficulties:

- recognizing letters
- communicating the alphabet
- reading basic sign words

Mr. Derrick discusses the issue with a special education teacher. Which of the following is the most appropriate step for a special education teacher to recommend as part of the pre-referral process?

- A. Continue instruction as normal and continue to monitor progress and revert back in 2 weeks.
- B. Involve the school psychologist to see if any non-academic issues are causing the difficulty in reading.
- C. Administer an informal diagnostic reading assessment to assess specific problem areas.
- D. Contact the parents to inform them about the issue and get permission to administer a test to determine any learning disabilities.

Answer:

QUESTION 74

An fifth-grade student has behavioral issues. He desires to stand in front of the line all the time. What can the teacher do to prevent temper tantrums?

- A. have him stand at the end of the line to teach him a lesson
- B. have him rotate standing in front of the line, which gives other students an opportunity to be in front of the line
- C. allow him to stand in the front when he desires to
- D. put him in the middle of the line

Answer:

QUESTION 75

The Individuals with Disabilities Education Improvement Act (IDEA):

- A. forces federal government to provide federal funding for early childhood programs
- B. requires states to create early intervention programs
- C. requires schools to have funding for improving technology for early childhood special education students
- D. requires states to provide data to the federal government on student progress in core academic areas

Answer:

QUESTION 76

In gym, James is unable to walk across a balance beam. Which of the following is the best option to undertake?

- A. place tape next to the beam and have him walk on the tape
- B. defer activity to the latter part of the year
- C. have him write how others completed activity
- D. have him watch video of kids walking across a balance beam

Answer:

QUESTION 77

A description of the student's current academic achievement level and functional performance is required by:

    A. Daily Assessment Records
    B. IEP
    C. IFSP
    D. 504 Plan

Answer:

QUESTION 78

Environmental factors play a significant factor in cognitive development of young children with learning disabilities. Which of the following has shown to have significant influence in cognitive development?

    A. caregiver-child interaction
    B. child-child interaction
    C. parent-teacher interaction
    D. number of family members in the home

Answer:

QUESTION 79

A policy change has been announced at a school that impacts special education services. The special education teachers feel that the change will likely reduce their ability to provide necessary services to students with disabilities. The best action for the special education teachers is to:

    A. communicate the pros and cons of the policy to provide a balance view
    B. communicate the negative impact the change will likely cause
    C. start a petition to prevent the change from being implemented
    D. develop a plan to work around the policy to support the students

Answer:

QUESTION 80

Mark is a new student who is handicapped, and he has been placed in a fifth-grade classroom. Jimmy and John are making fun of Mark. As a teacher, the best approach to take is:

- A. inform all students that we are friends at school
- B. punish Jimmy and John
- C. inform Jimmy and John that it is mean to make fun of others
- D. engage Mark with students who are more positive

Answer:

QUESTION 81

The Family Educational Rights and Privacy Act of 1974 give parents/guardians of a minor who is getting special needs services the right to:

- A. remove their child from standardize exams
- B. obtain educational records to share with non-school individuals
- C. select special education services
- D. opt out of IEP meetings

Answer:

QUESTION 82

- walks forward along the edge of a sandbox, watching feet
- jumps off a low step, landing on two feet
- jumps over small objects

Which of the following age group is being identified above?

- A. 1 – 2 years
- B. 2 – 3 years
- C. 3 – 4 years
- D. 4 – 5 years

Answer:

QUESTION 83

Which is the best way to teach hand-eye coordination to a student with developmental delays?

    A. dribble a basketball
    B. bean bag toss
    C. riding a tricycle
    D. obstacle course

Answer:

QUESTION 84

IDEA covers which of the following disabilities from birth:

    I.   cerebral palsy
    II. visual impairment
    III. down syndrome
    IV. hearing impairment

    A. I and III
    B. II and IV
    C. I and II
    D. III and IV

Answer:

QUESTION 85

A teacher overhears a student picking on another student. The student says "you look very ugly with glasses." What is the best phrase for the teacher to say to the student doing the picking?

    A. we treat all of our classmates with respect
    B. we all look different, it's no need to point it out
    C. we do not want to be mean to others
    D. glasses are to help people see better

Answer:

QUESTION 86

A student is frustrated with building a tower because he desires to build it like his classmate has. What should the teacher do?

A. help the student build the tower just like his classmate has
B. help the student find his own way to build the tower
C. help the student understand all towers are different
D. help the student visualize the tower

Answer:

QUESTION 87

_____ refers to a child's ability to recognize, express, and manage his/her feelings and to comprehend and react to the feeling of others.

A. social development
B. emotional development
C. physical development
D. behavioral development

Answer:

QUESTION 88

Ana is a third-grade student with cerebral palsy. She has trouble using handheld writing tools for legible writing. Which of the following best explains this condition?

A. underdeveloped fine-motor skills
B. inability to recognize appropriate writing tools
C. lack of experience in using writing tools
D. difficulty processing information

Answer:

QUESTION 89

_____ generally is the first communication behavior in a typical developing infant.

   A. Hearing a familiar voice and smiling
   B. Imitating word sounds
   C. Engaging in hitting
   D. Babbling when worried

Answer:

QUESTON 90

What is one way a teacher can avoid confusion and delays caused by activity transitions?

   A. increase voice during transitions to ensure everyone is listening
   B. establish a daily schedule with clear objectives
   C. ask students to stop all work and put down their pencils
   D. provide incentives for timely transitions

Answer:

QUESTION 91

Mrs. Manning is a special education middle school teacher. Which of the following situations would be most appropriate for Mrs. Manning to use norm-referenced testing?

   A. decide if a student should be promoted to the next grade level
   B. decide if a group is ready to move to the next activity
   C. to confirm a diagnosis regarding special needs
   D. identify strengths and weaknesses of students

Answer:

QUESTION 92

Bart is a 9-year-old ADHD student who has been informed he has diabetes. He is undergoing the process of learning to manage diabetes, which includes insulin injections, monitoring sugar levels, diet, and exercise. Of the following areas, which will be affected the most by diabetes?

- A. fine motor skills
- B. language development
- C. relationship with peers
- D. academic achievement

Answer:

QUESTION 93

Mr. Jordon's goal is to introduce a multicultural theme in his preschool classroom with special education students. What will be the best strategy to do that?

- A. put pictures of different cultures around the classroom
- B. read stories from different parts of the world during circle time
- C. read books of different cultures in the classroom
- D. use different kind of cultural dolls

Answer:

QUESTION 94

- I. parents
- II. regular education teacher(s)
- III. special education teacher(s)

According to IDEA 2004, an IEP team meeting consists of which of the following from above?

- A. I and II
- B. I and III
- C. II and III
- D. I, II, and III

Answer:

QUESTION 95

Emily is a first grade special education teacher. She is deciding on what music to play to her students. She should:

A. tell them this is her first year and the class will all learn together
B. survey students on what they like to listen to
C. show various music videos
D. play different types of grade appropriate music

Answer:

QUESTION 96

A student asks her teacher to help her write her name because she can't hold the pencil. The teacher should:

A. have her use a pencil grip
B. have her do hand strengthening activities
C. have her practice writing her name in sand
D. write her name for her all the time

Answer:

QUESTION 97

Mrs. Barbara is seeking to teach listening skills to her second-grade students. What is the best approach for her to take?

A. play a guessing game
B. call on students not participating
C. reading different stories and having the students answer questions about the story
D. state a list of nonsense words and have the students repeat them back

Answer:

QUESTION 98

Jake is a student with cerebral palsy. He most likely struggles in the developmental area of:

A. neurological
B. adaptive
C. muscular
D. hearing

Answer:

QUESTION 99

An early childhood teacher wants to support a student with cognitive impairment to become more independent in managing schoolwork. Which of the following would likely be the most effective first step for this goal?

A. have a check off list to document completed assignments
B. discuss with the student's parents on the goal
C. have the student periodically write in calendar upcoming assignments
D. provide the student with incentives for getting assignments done on time

Answer:

QUESTION 100

A special education student has been transitioned to a general education classroom. The teacher has noticed that the student is not behaving properly and disturbing other students even after the teacher has intervened multiple times. Which of the following is the next step the teacher should take?

A. continue to work with the student to get him to behave
B. review the transition plan and see if the plan has been followed as documented
C. have him go back to the special education classroom
D. consult with the special education teacher to seek the best option

Answer:

QUESTION 101

An elementary math teacher is seeking to find out if the students have mastered the instructional objectives at the end of the unit. What type of assessment is the best to use?

A. norm- referenced
B. achievement
C. diagnostic
D. placement

Answer:

QUESTION 102

Meg is a special education math teacher at a local elementary school. She is doing an activity with sticky notes. She has students put the number of individuals living in their homes on the sticky notes and place it on a horizontal line. Then, they take the sticky notes and arrange them from the most number of individuals living in homes to least number of individuals living in homes. What concept is the teacher aiming to support the students in understanding?

A. mean
B. mode
C. medium
D. range

Answer:

QUESTION 103

_____ are assessments that provide information on where an individual student's performance is in relation to his/her peers.

A. Formative assessments
B. Norm-referenced assessments
C. Criterion-referenced assessments
D. Subjective assessments

Answer:

QUESTION 104

Several special education students with mild disabilities are doing well in math class, but they are having difficulty on tests and quizzes, what should their teacher do?

A. find out their study habits and find lessons to support the students in studying better
B. plan a unit on study habits
C. see if there are patterns on the questions students are getting wrong
D. do review sessions before tests and quizzes

Answer:

QUESTION 105

A second-grade special education math teacher is having each student stand on a large sheet of one inch graph paper. Each student's partner outlines the student's foot by tracing around it. Afterwards, the students then count the number of squares enclosing the outline. Which of the following is math concept is best being exposed to the student with this activity?

A. area
B. perimeter
C. graphing
D. proportion

Answer:

QUESTION 106

Maggie's child has Down syndrome, and she has insisted to the special education teacher that she wants her child to go to a general education classroom. Maggie has communicated this via email, letters, and in-person. The teacher has responded in an appropriate manner that special education services are required under the law and per IEP recommendation. Maggie has come to the school to discuss this with the special education teacher and continues to insist that the child be placed in a general education classroom. Which of the following is the best action for the special education teacher to undertake?

A. firmly communicate to the parent that the student will remain in special education classes
B. inform the parent to home school the child as the child will remain in special education classes in the public school system
C. conduct meeting with the school counselor to communicate the pros of having the student remain in special education classes
D. place the child in a general education classroom with a special education paraprofessional

Answer:

QUESTION 107

Kate, a special education student, focuses better in the morning. How can Kate's teacher better instruct her?

A. direct instruction needs to be done in afternoon
B. direct instruction needs to be done in the morning
C. complete group activities in the morning
D. teach only during the morning

Answer:

QUESTION 108

Which of the following is a common development delay for individuals with Down syndrome?

A. language delay
B. social skill delay
C. muscular development
D. motor control delay

Answer:

QUESTION 109

The school sent out a notice not to bring lunches with peanut butter. Jake is a sixth-grade student who has brought a peanut butter sandwich for lunch. The teacher saw the sandwich immediately, when Jake took it out of his lunch box. What should the teacher do first?

A. call the school nurse in case someone has an allergic reaction
B. take the sandwich and throw it in a trash basket away from the students
C. have Jake sit away from the students to eat his sandwich
D. call Jake's parents to remind him to not bring lunch with peanut butter

Answer:

QUESTION 110

Jason is a six year old with mild developmental delays, and he is unable to control his behavior when he does not get his way. Which of the following is the most effective approach for prompting self discipline?

A. inform him of punishments for not behaving
B. tell him that life is not fair and he won't always get his way
C. role play appropriate ways to express feelings
D. show him a video of children reacting to situations

Answer:

QUESTION 111

A young, special education English Language Learner, from a diverse background will develop which of the following language skills first?

A. recognizing sight words
B. talking to other children
C. following directions for worksheets
D. completing writing tasks

Answer:

QUESTION 112

Which of the following abilities generally emerges first in childhood motor development?

A. running straight in one direction with some accuracy
B. performing forward rolls
C. hopping
D. using stairs

Answer:

QUESTION 113

Which of the following assessment is used to evaluate students with learning disabilities at the conclusion of an instructional period (ex. at the end of a unit)?

A. formative assessment
B. interim assessment
C. summative assessment
D. placement assessment

Answer:

QUESTION 114

Mr. Blake, a special education science teacher, is seeking to teach his students about various types of rocks (sedimentary, metamorphic, etc.). Of the following, which of the following best fosters critical thinking?

A. classifying rock samples
B. researching rocks
C. labeling diagrams of rocks
D. watching video on rocks

Answer:

QUESTION 115

An elementary education special education teacher is working on a lesson on the concept that change occurs in systems. Which of the following demonstrates teaching the concept using the scientific inquiry method?

   A. experimenting how long it would take an ice cup to melt on a hot day
   B. watching video on digestive and immune systems
   C. reading textbook chapter on growing crops
   D. comparing and contrasting two seasons with use of graphic organizers

Answer:

QUESTION 116

An eighth-year-old uses both English and Spanish languages at home. Discussing with the teacher, the grandfather expressed concerns that his child sometimes mixes up words between the two languages. Which of the following would be the best response for the teacher to provide the grandfather?

   A. document instances of the child mixing words to see if patterns exist
   B. inform the grandfather that this will continue for many years to come
   C. inform grandfather that this is common for the child's age
   D. conduct a formal assessment for placement of special education services

Answer:

QUESTION 117

Before assigning a new chapter in the textbook, a special education social studies teacher walks students through the chapter's headings and subheadings. Prior to reading the entire chapter, the teacher encourages the students to read the chapter's introduction and summary. In taking this approach, the teacher is increasing comprehension of a content-area text by helping the students

   A. establish background knowledge of the topic.
   B. determine what is most critical to take away from the reading.
   C. increase awareness of entire chapter.
   D. analyze multiple viewpoints and perspectives.

Answer:

Expl

QUESTION 118

What is the best question to ask about geography reasoning in second grade when walking through a street with houses, and then ending up on a street with several businesses?

    A. How long will it take to get back to the original destination?
    B. Why are houses and businesses located on different streets?
    C. Why do businesses have larger spaces than homes?
    D. Why are there more businesses than houses?

Answer:

QUESTION 119

Mr. Raymond has seen that John, who is claustrophobic and diagnosed with ADHD, has been the last person to turn in-class assignment 12 times in a row. His grades on the assignments are above average. What is the likely reason for John being the last person to turn in assignments?

    A. He double checks his work.
    B. He is shy to come up to the front.
    C. He does not want to come upfront while everyone is turning assignments.
    D. He is afraid someone might push him.

Answer:

QUESTION 120

A teacher verbally directs a six-year-old student to perform a series of four sequential activities, and, then she obverse the student's performance. This approach is best for detecting which of the following?

    A. behavioral issues
    B. auditory memory issues
    C. cognitive impairment
    D. motor skill issues

Answer:

QUESTION 121

A special education teacher is ignoring a student's IEP recommendation. In fact, the teacher has not even looked at the student's IEP. This is:

- A. illegal
- B. legal
- C. professionally wrong
- D. acceptable as long as the student is learning

Answer:

QUESTION 122

For the last two weeks, a teacher has been abruptly ending lessons as she is unable to finish teaching. The best approach is to:

- A. decrease the length of the lesson activity to complete on time
- B. increase the speed of teaching
- C. have students ask questions at the very end
- D. find a way to end the lessons in a smooth manner even if the lesson is not completed

Answer:

QUESTION 123

What kind of classroom instruction would a new teacher have to provide a student with Down syndrome?

- A. involve the student in free activities
- B. establish a more routine schedule
- C. give direct instruction
- D. provide individual instruction

Answer:

QUESTION 124

A special education, kindergarten, English Learner student spells the word found as "fawned". This is an example of:

A. self-generated words
B. pseudo-letter
C. pseudo-words
D. pseudo-sentence

Answer:

QUESTION 125

Which of the following is the best listening comprehension content for English Learners who have mastered basic structural forms but not vocabulary development?

A. vocabulary words to memorize
B. oral readings with accompanying pictures
C. television shows
D. flashcards

Answer:

Practice Exam - Correct Answer Sheet

Below is an optional answer sheet to use to document answers.

Question Number	Correct Answer	Question Number	Correct Answer	Question Number	Correct Answer	Question Number	Correct Answer	Question Number	Correct Answer
1	A	31	D	61	D	91	C	121	C
2	C	32	C	62	A	92	C	122	D
3	b	33	C	63	D	93	A	123	C
4	b	34	B	64	B	94	D	124	A
5	B	35	C	65	C	95	D	125	B
6	D	36	B	66	A	96	A		
7	B	37	D	67	C	97	D		
8	D	38	A	68	C	98	C		
9	A	39	B	69	A	99	A		
10	D	40	A	70	C	100	B		
11	D	41	B	71	C	101	B		
12	B	42	C	72	A	102	C		
13	B	43	B	73	C	103	B		
14	C	44	B	74	C	104	A		
15	A	45	C	75	B	105	A		
16	B	46	B	76	A	106	C		
17	C	47	C	77	B	107	B		
18	C	48	C	78	A	108	A		
19	B	49	B	79	B	109	B		
20	C	50	C	80	A	110	C		
21	C	51	D	81	B	111	B		
22	D	52	B	82	C	112	A		
23	B	53	A	83	B	113	C		
24	A	54	D	84	A	114	A		
25	A	55	B	85	A	115	A		
26	C	56	B	86	B	116	C		
27	C	57	A	87	B	117	B		
28	A	58	C	88	A	118	B		
29	B	59	C	89	A	119	C		
30	C	60	C	90	B	120	B		

NOTE: Getting approximately 80% of the questions correct increases chances of obtaining passing score on the real exam. This varies from different states and university programs.

This page is intentionally left blank.

Practice Exam Questions and Answers

QUESTION 1

Which of the following type of equipment would be best for a student with cerebral palsy to eat?

A. swivel spoon
B. small spoon
C. fork
D. right-angle spoon

Answer: A

Explanation: Swivel spoon keeps food on the utensil when turned at any angle, which are good for individuals with little or no muscle control.

QUESTION 2

How many days can a special education student be suspended?

A. 3 days
B. 5 days
C. 10 days
D. 15 days

Answer: C

Explanation: After 10 school days, under IDEA, students with disabilities must get educational services.

QUESTION 3

Jake is an eleventh grade student with a specific learning disability. He informs his special education teacher that he desires a career related to gardening. Which of the following is the best first step for the teacher to take to support the student's long term goal?

- A. provide brochures related to colleges and careers focusing on gardening
- B. have the student complete an interest inventory to define objectives in detail
- C. inform student to pursue education in agriculture
- D. help the student find a summer internship related to gardening

Answer: B

Explanation: The student has interest in gardening, which includes various aspects. To understand the student's interest and desires, an interest inventory to define objectives in detail will support the student in achieving long term goals. The student will be able to understand better what exactly within gardening he likes to undertake.

QUESTION 4

A parent made a request to do assessments for his child as the parent is concerned that his son might have ADHD. Which of the following procedures will likely increase accuracy in the results of the assessment?

- A. have two special education teachers administer the same assessment and compare results
- B. schedule several short testing sessions instead of one long session
- C. include hands on activities to engage the student
- D. inform the student a reward will be given at the completion of the assessment

Answer: B

Explanation: Choice A does not increase accuracy of the results; it is a way to confirm the results. Choice A is not normal practice and is only undertaken in extraordinary circumstances. Rewards should not be given when assessing learning disabilities as that can cause bias in the results. Choice C is a good option but does not address the attention part as Choice B does. Doing short sessions can result in more accurate results for individuals suspected to have ADHD.

QUESTION 5

    I.   phonology
    II.   morphology
    III.   semantics
    IV.   syntax
    V.   pragmatics

Which of the following correctly orders the levels of language?

A. I, II, III, IV, V
B. I, II, IV, III, V
C. V, IV, III, II, I
D. I, III, II, V, IV

Answer: B

Explanation: The levels of language are in the following order: phonology, morphology, syntax, semantics, and pragmatics.

QUESTION 6

Which of the following ages are the best to introduce effective play?

A. 0 to 1
B. 1 to 3
C. 3 to 4
D. 4 to 5

Answer: D

Explanation: Play therapy is a form of therapy primarily geared toward children, and this approach is best for age group 4 to 5. Children are encouraged to explore life events that may have an effect on current circumstances, in a manner and pace of the child's choosing.

QUESTION 7

Which of the following is NOT a written expression?

    A. vocabulary
    B. morphology
    C. content
    D. sentence structure

Answer: B

Explanation: Morphology is the study of the forms of words, which is not directly related to written expression as oppose to the other options.

QUESTION 8

Which of the following is NOT an example of low tech assistance device?

    A. pencil grip
    B. splint
    C. paper stabilizer
    D. voice synthesizers

Answer: D

Explanation: Voice synthesizers are considered high tech devices. Pencil grip, splint, and paper stabilizer are low tech assistance device.

QUESTION 9

A student with a stuttering problem has a communication disorder with which of the following?

    A. blending
    B. fluency
    C. articulation
    D. dialect

Answer: A

Explanation: Blending is when parts of two or more words combine to create a new word. If a student is having stuttering problem, the student is struggling with blending.

QUESTION 10

Which of the following is the best to use for a student with difficulty listening when communicating instructions?

- A. visual stimulant
- B. short and clear directions
- C. questions and answer approach
- D. positive reinforcement and role playing

Answer: D

Explanation: The student has difficulty hearing, so giving positive reinforcement will keep the student engaged. Role playing will keep the student to pay attention as well to the instruction.

QUESTION 11

What does the Council for Exceptional Children focus on?

- A. provide professional development for special education teachers
- B. support in the development of standards
- C. advance the success of children with exceptionalities
- D. all of the above

Answer: D

Explanation: The Council for Exceptional Children focus on providing professional development for special education teachers, supporting the development of standards, and advancing the success of children with exceptionalities.

QUESTION 12

Impairments in social perceptions, interaction, and nonverbal communication with no major cognitive delays are characterized by _____.

   A. ADHD
   B. Asperger syndrome
   C. Williams syndrome
   D. Down syndrome

Answer: B

Explanation: Impairments in social perceptions, interaction, and nonverbal communication with no major cognitive delays are characterized by Asperger syndrome.

QUESTION 13

A special education student has multiple disabilities, which include emotional disturbance and cognitive impairment. The student is in a general education classroom with a 1:1 special education consultant. The sitting is not enough to support the student. Which of the following is the next best level of support to provide the student?

   A. full time
   B. itinerant
   C. instruction afterschool
   D. alterative

Answer: B

Explanation: If the 1:1 special education consultant is not enough to support the student, the next best level of support is itinerant, which is support that travels place to place. The support will be able to monitor the student in and out of classes within the school day and also outside of school hours. This will allow developing a comprehensive plan to support the student during school.

QUESTION 14

A special education teacher uses various methods, strategies, resources, and technology to support diverse learners targeting strengths and weaknesses. Which of the following practices is the special education teacher implementing?

- A. technology-based learning
- B. direct instruction
- C. differentiated instruction
- D. targeted instruction

Answer: C

Explanation: Differentiated instruction is when teachers implement various methods, strategies, resources, and technology to tailor instruction to meet individual needs.

QUESTION 15

A fifth-grade student with a specific learning disability functions at a third-grade level in written expression. The student communicates when asked a question during class discussion, but he is unable to put ideas in writing. Which of the following is the best approach to facilitate the understanding of the student's learning when given a curriculum-based science test that includes writing an essay?

- A. allow the student to complete the test with oral responses
- B. give the student extra time to complete assignment
- C. help the student start off the essay
- D. give the student a multiple choice assignment

Answer: A

Explanation: The student is performing two levels below the appropriate grade level, so the best approach is to modify assessment to meet student's need. Giving extra time or starting the essay is not going to help the student to complete the assessment. Since the student is able to communicate well, the best approach is to have the student complete the test with oral responses. Doing so, the teacher will be able to assess the content being presented to the student.

QUESTION 16

Mr. Martin has a 12th-grade student with Oppositional defiant disorder (ODD), and the student's has the most difficulty in reacting to stressful situation and gets extremely negative. Which of the following is the best first treatment approach to take with this student?

    A. Parent-Management Training Programs
    B. Cognitive Problem-Solving Skills Training
    C. Social Skills Programs
    D. Medication

Answer: B

Explanation: Cognitive Problem-Solving Skills Training is to reduce inappropriate behaviors by teaching the child positive ways of responding to stressful situations. This approach allows students to see situations in multiple ways and respond appropriately.

QUESTION 17

James is a student with severe, multiple disabilities. Which of the following strategies is best to effectively elicit an orienting response from James?

    A. give partial answers to reach full answers
    B. use modeling to give examples
    C. slightly change familiar activities
    D. provide reward for reaching correct answers

Answer: C

Explanation: The student has severe, multiple disabilities, so the student is going to have difficulty in communicate accurate responses. The best way to obtain accurate response is to make slight modifications to activities the student is familiar with. This will increase the student's chances of providing answers that are correct along with provide the student with a comfortable environment to communicate.

QUESTION 18

Kevin is a ninth-grade student who is highly distractible individual with a learning disability. Which of the following is the best first step to take in developing a behavior management plan?

A. determine if there is a connection with distractibility and learning disability
B. determine factors that contribute to effective behavior
C. define attending behaviors in operational terms to achieve
D. review any previous behavior management plan

Answer: C

Explanation: The first step is to understand the behavior that needs to be achieved. This step is taken before creating goals, objectives, or assessments.

QUESTION 19

Which of the following is the best instructional strategy for assisting students with fine-motor impairments to master the skills needed to dress?

A. provide repeated opportunities to observe
B. give repeated opportunities to apply the skills
C. give opportunities to dress and undress dolls
D. provide repeated opportunities to identify clothing

Answer: B

Explanation: The best way to learn fine-motor impairments to master the skills needed to dress is to have repeated opportunities to apply the skills.

QUESTION 20

A ninth-grade special education teacher is seeking to support a student who is:

- new to the United States
- English language learner
- diagnosed with orthopedic impairment
- meeting classroom expectations
- reluctant to response to oral questions from teacher questions
- willingly interacts with students during learning activities
- unwilling to interact with the teacher

Which of the following is the first question to answer to support the student's learning?

A. Is the student's disability impacting his development of English skills?
B. Is the student placed in the right grade level?
C. Is he accustomed to different teaching practices from his home country?
D. Does he have an IEP?

Answer: C

Explanation: The issue is the student is not comfortable when the teacher is working with the student. As a result, the best question to understand is if teaching practices in his home culture differ from those of United States' school.

QUESTION 21

A 10th-grade student with an intellectual disability is enrolled in a school-based training program to developing job skills. The student is first required to do an activity measuring speed and accuracy of sorting. Which of the following best describes the activity?

- A. criterion-referenced test
- B. norm-referenced test
- C. performance-based assessment
- D. scaled assessment

Answer: C

Explanation: Performance-based assessment represents a set of strategies for obtaining knowledge, skills, and work habits through the performance of tasks that are meaningful and engaging to students.

QUESTION 22

Compared to peers without disability, a 17-year-old student with a mild intellectual disability is likely to have more struggles with which of the following tasks?

- A. greeting individuals arriving at open house
- B. communicating with peers during lunch
- C. completing three-step task for science experiment
- D. recalling a set of steps to complete a science experiment informed by the teacher a few minutes earlier

Answer: D

Explanation: Mild intellectual disability is an impairment of cognitive skills, adaptive life skills, and social skills. A student with mild intellectual disability is likely to have difficulty in recalling a set of steps to complete a science experiment informed by the teacher a few minutes earlier.

QUESTION 23

A special education teacher is planning to teach a seventh-grade student with autism to brush his teeth and comb his hair. Which of the following instructional methods is most effective for teaching these skills?

   A. sequencing chaining
   B. backward chaining
   C. peer modeling
   D. forward chaining

Answer: B

Explanation: Backward chaining is a method working backward from the goal(s). Backward chaining is a chaining procedure that begins with the last element in the chain and proceeds to the first element. This approach is used for teaching skills that consist of a chain of separate steps performed in the unchanged order.

QUESTION 24

Which of the following is the best approach for an inexperienced special education teacher to learn about instructional practice?

   A. use a website that ends with .gov or .org
   B. ask a general education teacher
   C. use college textbook
   D. an educational blog

Answer: A

Explanation: Of the choices, the best option is A. Using websites with .gov or.org can provide reliable information.

QUESTION 25

A tenth-grade student is defiant, spiteful, and negative. The student is showing signs of
_____.

- A. ADHS
- B. ODD
- C. ADD
- D. OCD

Answer: B

Explanation: Oppositional defiant disorder (ODD) is one of a group of behavioral disorders called disruptive behavior disorders (DBD). ODD signs include defiant, spiteful, hostility, and negativity.

QUESTION 26

A tenth-grade student with a mild intellectual disability and dyscalculia is getting instruction in daily living skills. Of the following tasks, which is likely the most difficult for this student?

- A. counting up to five
- B. recognizing common objects
- C. applying previous knowledge to different environment
- D. identifying time

Answer: C

Explanation: A tenth-grade student with mild intellectual disability and dyscalculia should be able to count to five. Recognizing time and identifying time is not going to be difficult for a tenth-grade student with mild intellectual disability and dyscalculia. The most difficult task is applying previous knowledge to different environment.

QUESTION 27

A prescribed stimulant medication for ADHD includes common side effects of
_____.

    A. poor circulation
    B. inability to concentrate
    C. loss of appetite
    D. low blood pressure

Answer: C

Explanation: Of the choices, loss of appetite is a common side effect of a prescribed stimulant medication for ADHD.

QUESTION 28

Parents of a secondary student are meeting with the special education teacher. Which of the following strategies will foster effective communication during the conference?

    A. use direct language without technical terms
    B. engage in discussion related to activities done during the weekend
    C. ask parents to write questions before coming to the meeting
    D. have research articles on topics of concern that might surface

Answer: A

Explanation: The most effective way to communicate with during a conference is to use direct language without technical terms. Technical terms can confuse some parents, which will not foster good communication.

QUESTION 29

A special education teacher has four students in a group, and two of the students have specific learning disabilities. The teacher is having difficulty getting one student with learning disability to learn adding fractions. Which of the following is the best approach to get the students to learn adding fraction?

- A. additional practice
- B. one-on-one instruction
- C. use blocks
- D. use alternative method

Answer: B

Explanation: If the student is not able to learn adding fraction in a group of four students, then the best approach is to give one-on-one instruction to target students' need.

QUESTION 30

Which of the following math skills is most likely the easiest for a student with autism to acquire?

- A. adding numbers
- B. subtracting numbers
- C. reciting numbers in order
- D. writing numbers

Answer: C

Explanation: Many children with autistic spectrum condition show good ability in reciting and ordering numbers as the number system is a sequence, which fits nicely with the way children with autism learn and remember facts.

QUESTION 31

Why is math so difficult to learn for individuals at early age with ADHD?

   A. includes numbers
   B. includes multistep procedures
   C. takes time to complete problems
   D. requires memory, problem solving and organizing skills

Answer: D

Explanation: Mastering math skills can be complex at early age, especially those with ADHD as math requires several processes including memory, problem solving, and organizing skills.

QUESTION 32

Mr. Sheppard, a fifth-grade special education science teacher, is working with autistic students to spot simple machines in daily surroundings. Which of the following daily objects would be the best example of a lever?

   A. a ramp
   B. skateboard
   C. hammer
   D. desk

Answer: C

Explanation: The daily object that best shows example of a lever is a hammer.

QUESTION 33

Carla is the mother of Susan, who attends secondary education school. Susan has come home multiple times with scratches inflicted by another student, Martha. Which of the following best indicates the most inappropriate response for the teacher to undertake along with what action the teacher should undertake?

A. The teacher would be wrong to tell the parent that Martha and Susan had difficulty working together that day. The teacher would be right in informing the parent that she will monitor both students closely going forward and report back.
B. The teacher would be wrong to generalize that there might have been some provocative verbal communication, which resulted in the scratches. The teacher would be right to take action by involving the principal and recommending appropriate punishments.
C. The teacher would be wrong to suggest that Martha's action resulted due to issues occurring in her family. The teacher would be right in informing the parent that she will monitor both students closely going forward and report back.
D. The teacher would be wrong to generalize that there might have been some provocative verbal communication, which resulted in the scratches. The teacher would be right in informing the parent that she will monitor both students closely going forward and report back.

Answer: C

Explanation: The teacher does not have the knowledge of the family to suggest the scratches were due to issues occurring in her family. The teacher needs to monitor both students closely and report further issues.

QUESTION 34

Mary, an eighth grade special education teacher, is alarmed by one student's appearance and behavior as the perceptions seems that she has been physically abused at home. According to state and federal law, the teacher is required to immediately:

A. inform the school nurse to allow him or her to take appropriate action
B. ensure her suspicions are reported in compliance with state/federal law and requirements
C. contact the parents to inform them of the situation
D. ask indirect questions to confirm suspicions and proceed in contacting law enforcement

Answer: B

Explanation: State and federal law require that suspicion of child abuse be reported to appropriate agencies. The teacher has suspected abuse and it is required for the teacher to report the suspicions, so necessary individuals can investigate.

QUESTION 35

   I. all special education students in America
   II. students with severe disabilities
   III. students eligible for special education in public schools

IEP is/are required for:

A. I only
B. I and II
C. II and III
D. I, II, and III

Answer: C

Explanation: Students in private schools are not mandated to have IEPs, which eliminates options that include I.

QUESTION 36

A first-grade teacher designed an activity using balls for her six students with specific learning disabilities. The teacher marks off a space and provides balls of different sizes, materials, and color. Pairs of students are allowed 30 minutes to explore the balls and 15 minutes to discuss the question, "How did the balls roll?" Which of the following type of teaching is being implemented in this activity?

- A. circular instruction
- B. inquiry instruction
- C. direct instruction
- D. indirect instruction

Answer: B

Explanation: Inquiry-based teaching involves the curiosity of students and the scientific method to enhance the development of critical thinking skills. Inquiry-based teaching starts with questions, problems, or scenarios.

QUESTION 37

Fourth-grade students with learning disabilities have been identifying planets in the solar system and their position in relation to the Sun. Which of the following culminating activities would be the best for assessment purposes of the students' learning?

- A. students complete a final assessment on the unit topic
- B. students complete a exit-slip on the unit topic
- C. students complete a report on the unit topic
- D. students complete a science fair project on the unit topic

Answer: D

Explanation: A culminating activity is an advance, summary that is carried out with a high degree of independence. The best option is a science fair project on the unit topic.

QUESTION 38

A special education math teacher has a student with IEP to complete classroom assignments independently 85% of the time. The special education teacher is modeling and doing group activities to teach and engage the student. Which of the following methods is the best to help the student work with increasing independence?

A. fading
B. independence
C. ignoring
D. self-grading

Answer: A

Explanation: Fading is the best approach to increase independence without doing abruptly.

QUESTION 39

A special education teacher works with several eighth-grade students with specific learning disabilities in reading. In addition, these students do not have the desire to read for pleasure. Which of the following methods is best to foster students' interest in independent reading?

A. establish a reading program that rewards students
B. provide students with reading material tailored to their reading abilities
C. give students more opportunity to spend time in library
D. establish a goal for the class to reach in regards to reading books

Answer: B

Explanation: Rewarding students that are not interested is not the best approach to ensure long term interest in reading. Giving students reading material related to individual abilities will better engage students to read, ultimately fostering independent reading.

QUESTION 40

- delay in counting
- difficulty in memorizing arithmetic facts
- delay in addition

The above are most likely associated with which of the following disability?

A. dyscalculia
B. acalculia
C. dyslipidemia
D. dyscalculia

Answer: A

Explanation: Dyscalculia is severe difficulty in making arithmetical calculations, as a result of brain disorder.

QUESTION 41

A teacher plans to inform the parents of their child's results on an evaluation. The child is a fifth-grade student with ADD. To ensure the information is effectively communicated, the teacher should:

A. develop a chart summarizing the results
B. use non-technical language that the parents will understand
C. provide background information on the assessment
D. show parents worksheets completed by the student

Answer: B

Explanation: The parents might not know the meaning of all the technical terms associated with assessments. The best approach is to use language that is aligned to the audience. In this case, using non-technical language is the best approach.

QUETSION 42

A special education teacher has a student with epilepsy. If the student has a seizure in class, the teacher should first:

- A. call for the school nurse to help
- B. move the other students to another room
- C. remove objects located around the student
- D. gently restrain the student

Answer: C

Explanation: The first step is to ensure the student does not get hurt, so the teacher needs to remove objects around the student that can possibly cause injury.

QUESTION 43

What is typical way for a pre-kindergarten autistic child to communicate with a teacher?

- A. verbal
- B. non-verbal
- C. written
- D. communication board

Answer: B

Explanation: A typical way for a pre-kindergarten autistic child to communicate with a teacher is non-verbal.

QUESTION 44

James is a tenth-grade student with a Functional Behavioral Assessment (FBA). He has unexpectedly become physically aggressive with others in school. To ensure effective intervention, which of the following should be done first by the IEP team?

- A. interview peers and teachers
- B. define behavior in measureable terms
- C. predict reasoning for changes in behavior
- D. develop a plan to collect data

Answer: B

Explanation: Having the behavior defined in measurable terms will allow concrete information when evaluating effectiveness of the intervention plan.

QUESTION 45

I. handles a book properly
II. awareness that reading is done from left to right
III. awareness that words are put together to convey information

The above are signs that demonstrate a child is developing skills associated with:

A. phonics
B. fluency
C. concept of print
D. ability to read

Answer: C

Explanation: All signs indicate the student is developing the skills associated with the concept of print. The answer is not Choice D as the options contain the word "awareness." Awareness indicates early stages of reading developing, which makes the answer concept of print.

QUESTION 46

A special education teacher moves his finger continuously along each line of the text as he reads a Big Book. This approach is most useful for supporting students' understanding the concept that:

A. print can be big and small
B. print has directionality
C. sentence consist of words
D. words are decodable

Answer: B

Explanation: Using fingers show that there is direction in print (reading books). The keyword in the question is "moves" which is linked to direction (involving movement).

QUESTION 47

   I. Diagnostic assessment allow teachers to map out a route, using existing knowledge to build upon.
   II. Response to Intervention is an approach for the early identification and support of students with learning and behavior needs.
   III. Screening assessments are used to determine whether students are ready to end a course.

Of the above, which of the following is/are correctly stated?

A. I only
B. II only
C. I and II
D. I, II, and III

Answer: C

Explanation: Screening assessments are used to determine whether students are ready to enter a course.

QUESTION 48

Which of the following assessment is used to evaluate student learning at the conclusion of an instructional period (ex. at the end of a unit)?

A. formative assessment
B. interim assessment
C. summative assessment
D. placement assessment

Answer: C

Explanation: Summative assessment is used to evaluate student learning at the conclusion of an instructional period. Formative assessment is an in-process evaluation of learning that is normally administered multiple times during a unit or course. Placement assessment is used to place students in courses. Interim assessment is used to see if students are in the right track for learning.

QUESTION 49

A teacher is promoting the idea of introducing fundamental structure of all subject areas in the early years of individual's education and revisiting them in more complex forms over time. This idea is called:

A. complex curriculum
B. spiral curriculum
C. reciprocal curriculum
D. instructional curriculum

Answer: B

Explanation: The question states the teacher wants to introduce the subject areas in early years and revisit them. The answer choice needs to relate to coming back to the subject areas. Spiral is related to a circle, and a circle comes back to the original starting point. Spiral curriculum is when students will see the same topics throughout their school career, with each encounter increasing in complexity and reinforcing previous learning.

QUESTION 50

I. summary of the student's process in vocational skills
II. summary of the present level of development
III. statement of major expected outcomes

Which of the following is/are included in an Individual Family Service Plan?

A. I only
B. I and II
C. II and III
D. I, II, and III

Answer: C

Explanation: Individual Family Service Plan includes a summary of the present level of development and a statement of major expected outcomes.

QUESTION 51

A special education teacher is displaying equipment to show various types of objects found in a lab. One student starts playing with one of the equipment. What is the best type of social discipline action to be taken?

    A. remove the student from the classroom and explain to other students this behavior is unacceptable
    B. use the equipment student has next in explaining the equipment of the lab
    C. place the student away from the equipment
    D. move closer to the student to let him know the instructor is aware of the behavior

Answer: D

Explanation: The best type of social discipline action to take is to move closer to the student to let him know the instructor is aware of the behavior.

QUESTION 52

Which of the following activities would be the most meaningful science experience for first grade students with mild learning disabilities?

    A. participating in hands-on instruction from a textbook
    B. engaging in self-generated, open-ended investigations
    C. viewing an educational video with the class
    D. conducting an experiment in lab

Answer: B

Explanation: Option A is not the best option because of the aspect of using textbook, which is not grade appropriate for first graders. Option C is not meaningful. Option D is not grade appropriate. Option B is meaningful as it requires students to think, and the activity is grade appropriate.

QUESTION 53

Mr. Mark, a special education teacher, has a student that has been diagnosed with a disease, and the student will be missing school frequently. The student is in the process of being tested to confirm the prognosis. In class, Mr. Mark's best action to take is:

A. to observe the student carefully and ask the student frequently if she is doing well
B. to inform the student that she can go to the nurse at anytime with permission
C. to send reports to the parents on how the student is doing during class
D. to assist her in understanding the disease and let her know she has the support of her teacher

Answer: A

Explanation: The student has a disease that can cause complications because the prognosis has not been confirmed. The best action to take is to observe the student and ask the student if she is doing okay. This is a direct impact to supporting the student to ensure action is taken in case something goes wrong. Choice B seems like another possible correct action, but it is not the best approach. Informing the student that she can go to the nurse at anytime is not as impactful as observing the student. Choice C has no direct impact in supporting the student in the classroom. Choice D is not the best option because the teacher may not be qualified to explain the disease.

QUESTION 54

Blake is a new student from another state, and he has separation anxiety. At the beginning of class during circle time, he does not want to let his father go. The best action for the teacher is to:

A. have the father come visit Blake a couple of times per day
B. have the father remain with Blake for 15 minutes and, then, ask him to leave
C. have the father participate in circle time, and when Blake is involved, have the parent sneak out of the room
D. introduce Blake to two friends and ask him to sit between them and engage in a discussion

Answer: D

Explanation: Having the father come visit a couple of times per day is not normal practice, so A is not the correct answer. Choice B involves the father leaving abruptly, which will not support the student's separation anxiety. Choice C seems like a good option, but because it asks for the father to participate in the circle time, Choice C is not the best option. Introducing Blake to several friends and having him engage with them will distract Blake and allow the parent to leave.

QUESTION 55

A special education preschool teacher, Mrs. Martin, plays a game with her students in which she says a familiar word and her students respond by repeating and drawing out each individual sound. For example, when Mrs. Martin says the word "kiss", the students will say "kkkkiiiissss." This activity is an oral language activity that involves phonemic segmentation. This activity most likely supports which of the following future literacy skills?

- A. writing letters
- B. spelling
- C. recognizing
- D. word definitions

Answer: B

Explanation: The students are repeating the words but drawing out each individual sounds. This will support students in spelling out words in the future. Writing is not being done here, so Choice A is eliminated. Recognizing is not a literacy skill, so Choice C is eliminated. Choice D is not grade appropriate.

QUESTION 56

- I. carries toys or objects while walking
- II. kicks a ball forward
- III. jumps in place
- IV. throws a ball overhand with some accuracy

Of the above gross motor skills, which of the following are characterized as actions taken by a typical 18 to 36 month old child?

- A. I and II
- B. I and III
- C. I and IV
- D. II and IV

Answer: B

Explanation: Carrying toys and objects while walking and jumping in place are actions taken by 18 to 36 month old children. Kicking a ball forward and throwing a ball overhand with accuracy are actions taken by 36 to 60 month old children.

QUESTION 57

During a parent teacher conference, a seventh-grade special education teacher informs the parents of a student that their child likely has ADHD. What did the teacher do wrong?

A. The teacher did nothing wrong.
B. The teacher did not administer an informal assessment to determine if the student had ADHD.
C. The teacher did not use an appropriate individual to test, confirm, and diagnose the student.
D. The teacher informed the parents of a "likely" scenario.

Answer: A

Explanation: The keyword in the question is "likely", which means the teacher is not confirming or diagnosing the student with ADHD. This teacher is specialized in special education, so she has the expertise to indicate her opinion, so answer choice C and D are out. Also, parents would need to give permission to allow any evaluation of specific learning disabilities. Informal assessments are not needed to determine ADHD. The teacher did nothing wrong by informing the parents that their child likely has ADHD.

QUESTION 58

Of the following, early childhood students typically develop which expressive language skills last?

A. use of four words to make a short sentence
B. use of few words to make a request
C. use of pronouns to indicate people
D. use of conjugations to link simple ideas

Answer: C

Explanation: Early childhood students using few words to communicate is one of the first expressive language skills, which eliminates A and B. Early childhood students learn to link ideas before learning the use of pronouns to indicate people. Moreover, using few words to communicate comes before learning how to use pronouns to indicate people.

QUESTION 59

Family Educational Rights and Privacy Action (FERPA) protect students' records at school institutions in America. Which of the following situations of a request to see a student's records will be approved?

A. A parent seeking to confirm a student's enrollment in the appropriate special education program.
B. A parent seeking to confirm a student's IEP is acceptable to ensure proper learning.
C. A parent questioning a student's placement for special education classes for the new school year.
D. A parent questioning a student's grades and requesting to see all assignment grades.

Answer: C

Explanation: Choice A does not require the need for academic records nor has anything to do with FERPA. Choice B is incorrect as IEP are provided and discussed with parents; FERPA does not address this. Choice C is correct as that is acceptable reason to view records. Choice D is incorrect as FERPA does not go into details about parents challenging student's grades.

QUESTION 60

Mr. Jon has been informed that a new student will be coming into his class. The student has special needs. Mr. Jon conducts a meeting with the special education instructor to review the goals in the new student's IEP. Which of the following describe Mr. Jon's responsibilities regarding the IEP goals?

A. ensuring that the goals are kept confidential
B. setting up an incentive approach to ensure goals are being accomplished
C. having activities in the classroom related to the IEP goals
D. selecting the most critical goals for planning lesson plans

Answer: C

Explanation: The teacher needs to include activities in the classroom related to IEP goals to give the student opportunities to attempt and achieve those goals.

QUESTION 61

A second grade teacher notices a child removing food from lunch and hiding it in his backpack. The teacher notices this behavior and discusses it with the student after class. In the discussion, the student mentions his father lost his job and that there is not much food to eat. Which of the following is the most appropriate first response for the teacher to take?

- A. contact the principal to develop a plan to ensure proper food is given to the student outside of the school
- B. contact Child Protective Services (CPS) to report possible neglect at home
- C. provide the student with food and snacks to take home going forward
- D. speak to the family about relevant community services and support during this difficult time

Answer: D

Explanation: The best action to take is to talk to the family and inform them of the support systems available. At this time, escalating this to the principal and CPS is unnecessary. Providing the student with food and snacks is not the right direction to proceed in.

QUESTION 62

Jake is a third grade student who has been diagnosed with a learning disability known as written expression. Of the following, which one is the least restrictive environment?

- A. an inclusion classroom
- B. a quite environment
- C. a separate-closed room
- D. a pull-out resource room

Answer: A

Explanation: The student's disability is "written expression", so interaction is needed to support the student. A general education inclusion classroom will allow the student to interact with peers while getting the necessary support from a general education instructor and a special education instructor.

QUESTION 63

Mrs. Perez teaches fourth grade students. There are 21 students, and three of the students have developmental delays. Which of the following provides Mrs. Perez with the necessary data to differentiate instruction for those three students?

A. discuss with co-teachers on previous methods used in the school
B. monitor students' progress to see what approaches are working
C. ask the students what approach has worked in the past
D. review previous performance records to understand strengths and weaknesses

Answer: D

Explanation: Having an understanding of students' strengths and weaknesses allows the teacher to tailor the lessons to students' needs. All students are different and relying solely on co-teacher discussion will not be the best approach to support students, so choice A is eliminated. The students are in first grade and have developmental delays, so asking the students is not the best approach. Choice B will not allow the teacher to tailor the current lesson to the students' needs; the data might be useful in future planning.

QUESTION 64

Which of the following hand to eye coordination games best fits three to four year olds in a classroom?

A. hide and seek
B. put a circle on board and ask students to throw a rubber ball inside the circle
C. have someone throw a ball and have another child hit the ball with a bat
D. build a structure with blocks

Answer: B

Explanation: Choice A and D have no connection to hand and eye coordination. Choice B is the answer as the students throw a rubber ball inside the circle testing the precision of hand to eye coordination. Choice C does not do that as someone will have to throw the ball, and using a bat in a classroom is not the best approach.

QUESTION 65

   I. a portfolio
   II. an intelligence test
   III. an adaptive behavior scale

Of the above, which of the following is/are formal assessment(s)?

A. I and II
B. I and III
C. II and III
D. I, II, and III

Answer: C

Explanation: A portfolio is an informal assessment. An intelligent test and adaptive behavior scale are formal assessments.

QUESTION 66

   I. a chromosomal disorder
   II. mother exposed to lead during pregnancy
   III. vaccination

Of the above, which is/are direct cause(s) of Down syndrome?

A. I only
B. II only
C. III only
D. I and II

Answer: A

Explanation: Down syndrome is a random error in cell division that occurs in the presence of an extra copy of chromosome 21. This disorder causes developmental and intellectual delays.

QUESTION 67

Of the following fine motor skills, which of the following does not characterize a 36 to 60 month old child?

    A. copies shapes and geometric shapes
    B. eats with utensils
    C. open doors, with assistance, by turning and pulling doorknobs
    D. manipulates small objects with ease

Answer: C

Explanation: Opening doors with assistance is typical for a child that is 18 to 36 month old. Another way to look at this question is that 36 to 60 month old children start to take basic actions without support. The only option that states assistance is Choice C.

QUESTION 68

Which of the following is the best learning objective for a special education class of third-grade learning about money?

    A. Students will be able to determine the value of fake money given to them.
    B. Students will be able to solve word problems asking them to solve for change left over.
    C. Students will be able to represent the value of money in fraction of a dollar.
    D. Students will be able to solve problems involving decimal operations.

Answer: C

Explanation: Option A is not the answer as value of money is introduced prior to third-grade. Option B is a learning target more appropriate for fourth grade level. Option D has nothing to do with money. Option C is grade appropriate and deals with money.

QUESTION 69

A fourth grade teacher notices that her students are having difficulty doing math problems involving fractions. What is the best first step for the teacher to undertake to support the students?

    A. have the students complete an assessment on basics of fractions
    B. assign the students extra practice on fractions for homework
    C. ask the students exactly what there are having difficulty with
    D. use direct teaching methods to show how to solve problems with fractions

Answer: A

Explanation: The students are in fourth grade and should be able to do math problems involving fractions. The best approach is to conduct an assessment on basic fractions to understand the gaps the students have regarding fractions. Option B does not support the students in their needs. Option C is good, but some students might not even know exactly what there are having difficulty with. Option D is a good option to undertake, but not the first step.

QUESTION 70

At the end of the unit on fraction, Mr. Locke, a special education math teacher, is seeking to determine what the students have learned. Which of the following assessments is the best to implement?

    A. authentic assessment
    B. standards-based assessment
    C. summative assessment
    D. norm-referenced assessment

Answer: C

Explanation: The goal of summative assessment is to assess student learning at the end of an instructional unit by comparing it against some standard or objective.

QUESTION 71

A child is coming into the classroom next year that is legally blind. What should the teacher request before the upcoming school year?

A. manipulative
B. communication board
C. speakers
D. smart board

Answer: C

Explanation: The student is blind, so the teacher should request something that will support the students learning. Since the student can hear, the best request is for speakers.

QUESTION 72

A special diet can be used to prevent learning disabilities in infants who are born with which of the following conditions?

A. phenylketonuria
B. down syndrome
C. fetal alcohol syndrome
D. none of the above

Answer: A

Explanation: Phenylketonuria is an inherited disorder that increases the levels of phenylalanine in the blood. Studies have indicated that a healthy whole-eating diet can support the prevention of learning disabilities in infants born with phenylketonuria. Diet consists of a phenylalanine-free medical formula and measured amounts of fruits, vegetables, bread, and pasta.

QUESTION 73

Mr. Derrick is a second-grade teacher. He is worried that one of his students, Bill, is having trouble acquiring basic reading skills. Bill has shown the following difficulties:

- recognizing letters
- communicating the alphabet
- reading basic sign words

Mr. Derrick discusses the issue with a special education teacher. Which of the following is the most appropriate step for a special education teacher to recommend as part of the pre-referral process?

A. Continue instruction as normal and continue to monitor progress and revert back in 2 weeks.
B. Involve the school psychologist to see if any non-academic issues are causing the difficulty in reading.
C. Administer an informal diagnostic reading assessment to assess specific problem areas.
D. Contact the parents to inform them about the issue and get permission to administer a test to determine any learning disabilities.

Answer: C

Explanation: Option A does not allow the teacher to support the student. Involving the school psychologist is unnecessary as nothing in the question indicates non-academic issues. The question states "pre-referral", so Choice D is not the best option. The best option in the "pre-referral" stage is to understand specific issues to proceed in discussing further with the special education teacher and/or parents.

QUESTION 74

An fifth-grade student has behavioral issues. He desires to stand in front of the line all the time. What can the teacher do to prevent temper tantrums?

  A. have him stand at the end of the line to teach him a lesson
  B. have him rotate standing in front of the line, which gives other students an opportunity to be in front of the line
  C. allow him to stand in the front when he desires to
  D. put him in the middle of the line

Answer: C

Explanation: The keywords in the question are "prevent temper tantrums". The student has behavioral issues, so disrupting his desire to be in the front of the line can cause him to act out. The best option is to allow him to stand in the front as he desires.

QUESTION 75

The Individuals with Disabilities Education Improvement Act (IDEA):

  A. forces federal government to provide federal funding for early childhood programs
  B. requires states to create early intervention programs
  C. requires schools to have funding for improving technology for early childhood special education students
  D. requires states to provide data to the federal government on student progress in core academic areas

Answer: B

Explanation: The Act does not force federal government to give funding, require schools to have funding for technology, or require states to provide data. The Act does require states to create early intervention programs.

QUESTION 76

In gym, James is unable to walk across a balance beam. Which of the following is the best option to undertake?

A. place tape next to the beam and have him walk on the tape
B. defer activity to the latter part of the year
C. have him write how others completed activity
D. have him watch video of kids walking across a balance beam

Answer: A

Explanation: Choice A is the only option that provides direct support in the gym and can support the student in accomplishing the task. Choice B is not the best option as no intervention is undertaken. Choice C is likely going to make the child feel uncomfortable as he will see others can do the activity and he can't. Watching a video is more for awareness purposes of walking on balance beam and that stage has passed; he attempted to walk but was unsuccessful. He needs intervention to support him in walking across the balance beam.

QUESTION 77

A description of the student's current academic achievement level and functional performance is required by:

A. Daily Assessment Records
B. IEP
C. IFSP
D. 504 Plan

Answer: B

Explanation: Individualized Education Program (IEP) requires a description of the student's current academic achievement level and functional performance.

QUESTION 78

Environmental factors play a significant factor in cognitive development of young children with learning disabilities. Which of the following has shown to have significant influence in cognitive development?

A. caregiver-child interaction
B. child-child interaction
C. parent-teacher interaction
D. number of family members in the home

Answer: A

Explanation: Choice C does not have any direct impact on young children. Interaction with family members is good support for learning disabilities but it is not the most significant. Child-child interaction is good but will not result in significant cognitive development as children are at the same learning level. Choice A provides the most significant influence to children to support them in cognitive development.

QUESTION 79

A policy change has been announced at a school that impacts special education services. The special education teachers feel that the change will likely reduce their ability to provide necessary services to students with disabilities. The best action for the special education teachers is to:

A. communicate the pros and cons of the policy to provide a balance view
B. communicate the negative impact the change will likely cause
C. start a petition to prevent the change from being implemented
D. develop a plan to work around the policy to support the students

Answer: B

Explanation: Best option is to be upfront about the change and communicate the negative impact to have the school reconsider the policy.

QUESTION 80

Mark is a new student who is handicapped, and he has been placed in a fifth-grade classroom. Jimmy and John are making fun of Mark. As a teacher, the best approach to take is:

A. inform all students that we are friends at school
B. punish Jimmy and John
C. inform Jimmy and John that it is mean to make fun of others
D. engage Mark with students who are more positive

Answer: A

Explanation: Choice D does not correct Jimmy and John for making fun, and they will likely continue to make fun of Mark. Choice B and C address Jimmy and John. To prevent others from taking the same action, this is not the best approach. The best approach is to inform all students that we are friends; this is a proactive approach that prevents other students from making fun of anyone and also addresses Jimmy and John.

QUESTION 81

The Family Educational Rights and Privacy Act of 1974 give parents/guardians of a minor who is getting special needs services the right to:

A. remove their child from standardize exams
B. obtain educational records to share with non-school individuals
C. select special education services
D. opt out of IEP meetings

Answer: B

Explanation: The Family Educational Rights and Privacy Act of 1974 give parents or guardians of a minor to obtain copies of students' academic records to share with individuals outside of the school system.

QUESTION 82

- walks forward along the edge of a sandbox, watching feet
- jumps off a low step, landing on two feet
- jumps over small objects

Which of the following age group is being identified above?

A. 1 – 2 years
B. 2 – 3 years
C. 3 – 4 years
D. 4 – 5 years

Answer: C

Explanation: Walking forward along a sandbox edge, jumping off low steps, and jumping over small objects are balancing skills shown by 3 – 4 year olds.

QUESTION 83

Which is the best way to teach hand-eye coordination to a student with developmental delays?

A. dribble a basketball
B. bean bag toss
C. riding a tricycle
D. obstacle course

Answer: B

Explanation: There is a direct connection to hand-eye coordination when tossing a bean bag.

QUESTION 84

IDEA covers which of the following disabilities from birth:

I. cerebral palsy
II. visual impairment
III. down syndrome
IV. hearing impairment

A. I and III
B. II and IV
C. I and II
D. III and IV

Answer: A

Explanation: Cerebral palsy and Down syndrome are conditions that cause severe learning disabilities and cognitive developmental issues. Cerebral palsy and Down syndrome are covered from birth under IDEA.

QUESTION 85

A teacher overhears a student picking on another student. The student says "you look very ugly with glasses." What is the best phrase for the teacher to say to the student doing the picking?

A. we treat all of our classmates with respect
B. we all look different, it's no need to point it out
C. we do not want to be mean to others
D. glasses are to help people see better

Answer: A

Explanation: Choice A gives the student doing the picking directions on how to interact with classmates; in a respectful manner. Choice B is a fact, but not the best statement as it does not create an environment to respect others. Choice C is similar to Choice A, but Choice A is more positive. Choice D does not resolve the issue of the student picking on another student.

QUESTION 86

A student is frustrated with building a tower because he desires to build it like his classmate has. What should the teacher do?

A. help the student build the tower just like his classmate has
B. help the student find his own way to build the tower
C. help the student understand all towers are different
D. help the student visualize the tower

Answer: B

Explanation: The student is frustrated, so the best approach is to help the student to build the tower. Choice A is not the best option as it does not allow the student to think to build the tower. Choice C and D do not have direct impact on the student in building the tower. Helping the student find his own way to build the tower will challenge the student and allow him to develop thinking skills, so the answer is B.

QUESTION 87

_____ refers to a child's ability to recognize, express, and manage his/her feelings and to comprehend and react to the feeling of others.

A. social development
B. emotional development
C. physical development
D. behavioral development

Answer: B

Explanation: Emotional development refers to a child's ability to recognize, express, and manage his/her feelings and to comprehend and react to the feeling of others.

QUESTION 88

Ana is a third-grade student with cerebral palsy. She has trouble using handheld writing tools for legible writing. Which of the following best explains this condition?

A. underdeveloped fine-motor skills
B. inability to recognize appropriate writing tools
C. lack of experience in using writing tools
D. difficulty processing information

Answer: A

Explanation: Cerebral palsy is linked to underdeveloped fine-motor skills, which can cause difficulty in using handheld writing tools for legible writing.

QUESTION 89

_____ generally is the first communication behavior in a typical developing infant.

- A. Hearing a familiar voice and smiling
- B. Imitating word sounds
- C. Engaging in hitting
- D. Babbling when worried

Answer: A

Explanation: Imitating and babbling occurs between four to six months of age. Around the second month of life, a child will smile when hearing a familiar voice.

QUESTON 90

What is one way a teacher can avoid confusion and delays caused by activity transitions?

- A. increase voice during transitions to ensure everyone is listening
- B. establish a daily schedule with clear objectives
- C. ask students to stop all work and put down their pencils
- D. provide incentives for timely transitions

Answer: B

Explanation: Having clear objectives and a schedule will support in time management and transition of activities. Giving incentives is not a long term solution, so Choice D is eliminated. Abruptly stopping all work will not always be the best approach, so Choice C is eliminated. Choice A does not directly solve the confusion and delays due to activity transitions.

QUESTION 91

Mrs. Manning is a special education middle school teacher. Which of the following situations would be most appropriate for Mrs. Manning to use norm-referenced testing?

- A. decide if a student should be promoted to the next grade level
- B. decide if a group is ready to move to the next activity
- C. to confirm a diagnosis regarding special needs
- D. identify strengths and weaknesses of students

Answer: C

Explanation: Norm-referenced tests report whether test takers performed better or worse than the average student. From the answer choices, the most appropriate use of norm-referenced testing is to confirm a diagnosis regarding special needs. The test will confirm if the student is performing better or worse than an average student.

QUESTION 92

Bart is a 9-year-old ADHD student who has been informed he has diabetes. He is undergoing the process of learning to manage diabetes, which includes insulin injections, monitoring sugar levels, diet, and exercise. Of the following areas, which will be affected the most by diabetes?

- A. fine motor skills
- B. language development
- C. relationship with peers
- D. academic achievement

Answer: C

Explanation: Of the areas, C is most likely to be affected by diabetes. Bart will have to undertake additional activities to manage diabetes, moist of which his peers do not undertake. Prior to eating, he will have to take insulin injections. He will have to exercise more than other individuals. All of these can likely impact his relationships with his peers.

QUESTION 93

Mr. Jordon's goal is to introduce a multicultural theme in his preschool classroom with special education students. What will be the best strategy to do that?

A. put pictures of different cultures around the classroom
B. read stories from different parts of the world during circle time
C. read books of different cultures in the classroom
D. use different kind of cultural dolls

Answer: A

Explanation: All answer choices relate to culture, but Choice A result in a long term impact and establishes a multicultural theme in his preschool classroom.

QUESTION 94

I. parents
II. regular education teacher(s)
III. special education teacher(s)

According to IDEA 2004, an IEP team meeting consists of which of the following from above?

A. I and II
B. I and III
C. II and III
D. I, II, and III

Answer: D

Explanation: Parents, at least one regular education teacher, and at least one special education teacher are needed in an IEP meeting.

QUESTION 95

Emily is a first grade special education teacher. She is deciding on what music to play to her students. She should:

A. tell them this is her first year and the class will all learn together
B. survey students on what they like to listen to
C. show various music videos
D. play different types of grade appropriate music

Answer: D

Explanation: The best option is D as it states grade appropriate music. Also, Choice D states different music, which is good to expose young children too. Choice A does not install confidence in the students if their teacher does not know music. Music videos are not grade appropriate. Surveys may not always be 100% reliable. Choice B also implies that majority of the votes will be the reason for selecting the music, which might not take into account all students. Also, students might not fill the survey out accurately.

QUESTION 96

A student asks her teacher to help her write her name because she can't hold the pencil. The teacher should:

A. have her use a pencil grip
B. have her do hand strengthening activities
C. have her practice writing her name in sand
D. write her name for her all the time

Answer: A

Explanation: Choice A is the only one that supports the student in holding the pencil. Choice C is a good option, but the issue resides in holding the pencil not writing her name.

QUESTION 97

Mrs. Barbara is seeking to teach listening skills to her second-grade students. What is the best approach for her to take?

A. play a guessing game
B. call on students not participating
C. reading different stories and having the students answer questions about the story
D. state a list of nonsense words and have the students repeat them back

Answer: D

Explanation: Choice D requires students to recite words that were communicated to them; this involves listening skills. Choice C involves listening skills, but is more targeted to comprehension skills.

QUESTION 98

Jake is a student with cerebral palsy. He most likely struggles in the developmental area of:

A. neurological
B. adaptive
C. muscular
D. hearing

Answer: C

Explanation: Cerebral palsy is a congenital disorder of movement, muscle tone, or posture.

QUESTION 99

An early childhood teacher wants to support a student with cognitive impairment to become more independent in managing schoolwork. Which of the following would likely be the most effective first step for this goal?

- A. have a check off list to document completed assignments
- B. discuss with the student's parents on the goal
- C. have the student periodically write in calendar upcoming assignments
- D. provide the student with incentives for getting assignments done on time

Answer: A

Explanation: Choice A keeps track of assignments completed and those not completed. Involving parents in this goal at this early stage is not necessary, so Choice B is eliminated. Choice C does not keep track of assignments completed, so that is not the answer. Keeping track of assignments completed is important as the student has a cognitive impairment disability. Choice D is not the first step to take.

QUESTION 100

A special education student has been transitioned to a general education classroom. The teacher has noticed that the student is not behaving properly and disturbing other students even after the teacher has intervened multiple times. Which of the following is the next step the teacher should take?

- A. continue to work with the student to get him to behave
- B. review the transition plan and see if the plan has been followed as documented
- C. have him go back to the special education classroom
- D. consult with the special education teacher to seek the best option

Answer: B

Explanation: A transition plan is the next step to review to ensure the recommendations are being followed. When transitioning to general education classrooms from special education, some individuals require additional attention. Since intervening on a regular basis is not working, reviewing the transition plan will be the next best step.

QUESTION 101

An elementary math teacher is seeking to find out if the students have mastered the instructional objectives at the end of the unit. What type of assessment is the best to use?

A. norm- referenced
B. achievement
C. diagnostic
D. placement

Answer: B

Explanation: An achievement test is a test of developed skill or knowledge.

QUESTION 102

Meg is a special education math teacher at a local elementary school. She is doing an activity with sticky notes. She has students put the number of individuals living in their homes on the sticky notes and place it on a horizontal line. Then, they take the sticky notes and arrange them from the most number of individuals living in homes to least number of individuals living in homes. What concept is the teacher aiming to support the students in understanding?

A. mean
B. mode
C. medium
D. range

Answer: C

Explanation: The teacher is having the students put the numbers in order from greatest to least. For mean, mode, and range, the need to put the numbers in order is not always necessary. Typically, for medium, the numbers are put in order to see which number is in the middle.

QUESTION 103

_____ are assessments that provide information on where an individual student's performance is in relation to his/her peers.

A. Formative assessments
B. Norm-referenced assessments
C. Criterion-referenced assessments
D. Subjective assessments

Answer: B

Explanation: Norm-referenced assessments are assessments that provide information on where an individual student's performance is in relation to his or her peers.

QUESTION 104

Several special education students with mild disabilities are doing well in math class, but they are having difficulty on tests and quizzes, what should their teacher do?

A. find out their study habits and find lessons to support the students in studying better
B. plan a unit on study habits
C. see if there are patterns on the questions students are getting wrong
D. do review sessions before tests and quizzes

Answer: A

Explanation: Students are doing well in class, but struggling on the quizzes and tests. This is an indication that the students are likely not studying correctly. The best option is for the teacher to find out about study habits and support them in studying the correct way.

QUESTION 105

A second-grade special education math teacher is having each student stand on a large sheet of one inch graph paper. Each student's partner outlines the student's foot by tracing around it. Afterwards, the students then count the number of squares enclosing the outline. Which of the following is math concept is best being exposed to the student with this activity?

A. area
B. perimeter
C. graphing
D. proportion

Answer: A

Explanation: The student is counting the squares that are enclosed in the outline, so the student is being exposed to the concept of area.

QUESTION 106

Maggie's child has Down syndrome, and she has insisted to the special education teacher that she wants her child to go to a general education classroom. Maggie has communicated this via email, letters, and in-person. The teacher has responded in an appropriate manner that special education services are required under the law and per IEP recommendation. Maggie has come to the school to discuss this with the special education teacher and continues to insist that the child be placed in a general education classroom. Which of the following is the best action for the special education teacher to undertake?

A. firmly communicate to the parent that the student will remain in special education classes
B. inform the parent to home school the child as the child will remain in special education classes in the public school system
C. conduct meeting with the school counselor to communicate the pros of having the student remain in special education classes
D. place the child in a general education classroom with a special education paraprofessional

Answer: C

Explanation: Maggie's behavior indicates she does not understand the importance of keeping her child in special education classes. Since Maggie has continued to communicate her desire to remove the child from special education classes, the teacher needs to involve the school counselor to support her in communicating the message. Choice A and B are too firm and negative, which can cause additional issues. Accepting the parent's desires of removing the student from special education classes without appropriate evaluation is not the approach to undertake.

QUESTION 107

Kate, a special education student, focuses better in the morning. How can Kate's teacher better instruct her?

- A. direct instruction needs to be done in afternoon
- B. direct instruction needs to be done in the morning
- C. complete group activities in the morning
- D. teach only during the morning

Answer: B

Explanation: Direct instruction requires the student to be completely focused. If the student is focused in the morning, the best approach is to do direct instruction in the morning.

QUESTION 108

Which of the following is a common development delay for individuals with Down syndrome?

- A. language delay
- B. social skill delay
- C. muscular development
- D. motor control delay

Answer: A

Explanation: Down syndrome is a genetic chromosome 21 disorder causing developmental and intellectual delays, which results in language delays. Individuals with Down syndrome have good social skills and empathy.

QUESTION 109

The school sent out a notice not to bring lunches with peanut butter. Jake is a sixth-grade student who has brought a peanut butter sandwich for lunch. The teacher saw the sandwich immediately, when Jake took it out of his lunch box. What should the teacher do first?

- A. call the school nurse in case someone has an allergic reaction
- B. take the sandwich and throw it in a trash basket away from the students
- C. have Jake sit away from the students to eat his sandwich
- D. call Jake's parents to remind him to not bring lunch with peanut butter

Answer: B

Explanation: The first step is to protect the students, so the teacher will want to throw the sandwich away.

QUESTION 110

Jason is a six year old with mild developmental delays, and he is unable to control his behavior when he does not get his way. Which of the following is the most effective approach for prompting self discipline?

    A. inform him of punishments for not behaving
    B. tell him that life is not fair and he won't always get his way
    C. role play appropriate ways to express feelings
    D. show him a video of children reacting to situations

Answer: C

Explanation: Choice A and B are not positive approaches to confront a six year old. Choice D is not involving the student directly and might not have a positive impact. Choice C allows the student to express feelings in an appropriate way, which is the correct answer.

QUESTION 111

A young, special education English Language Learner, from a diverse background will develop which of the following language skills first?

    A. recognizing sight words
    B. talking to other children
    C. following directions for worksheets
    D. completing writing tasks

Answer: B

Explanation: The keyword in the question is "first". The child is likely going to talk to other children at his or her grade level.

QUESTION 112

Which of the following abilities generally emerges first in childhood motor development?

    A. running straight in one direction with some accuracy
    B. performing forward rolls
    C. hopping
    D. using stairs

Answer: A

Explanation: Of the choices, in childhood motor development, running in one direction generally emerges first.

QUESTION 113

Which of the following assessment is used to evaluate students with learning disabilities at the conclusion of an instructional period (ex. at the end of a unit)?

A. formative assessment
B. interim assessment
C. summative assessment
D. placement assessment

Answer: C

Explanation: Summative assessment is used to evaluate student learning at the conclusion of an instructional period. Formative assessment is an in-process evaluation of learning that is normally administered multiple times during a unit or course. Placement assessment is used to place students in courses. Interim assessment is used to see if students are in the right track for learning.

QUESTION 114

Mr. Blake, a special education science teacher, is seeking to teach his students about various types of rocks (sedimentary, metamorphic, etc.). Of the following, which of the following best fosters critical thinking?

A. classifying rock samples
B. researching rocks
C. labeling diagrams of rocks
D. watching video on rocks

Answer: A

Explanation: The keywords in the question are "best" and "critical thinking". Having students classify rock samples will require them to think the most and involve them the most.

QUESTION 115

An elementary education special education teacher is working on a lesson on the concept that change occurs in systems. Which of the following demonstrates teaching the concept using the scientific inquiry method?

   A. experimenting how long it would take an ice cup to melt on a hot day
   B. watching video on digestive and immune systems
   C. reading textbook chapter on growing crops
   D. comparing and contrasting two seasons with use of graphic organizers

Answer: A

Explanation: Scientific inquiry method is when steps are taken to study the natural world and proposed explanations based on the evidence gathered. Experimenting involves taking steps. The experiment mentioned in Option A relates to the study of the natural world.

QUESTION 116

An eighth-year-old uses both English and Spanish languages at home. Discussing with the teacher, the grandfather expressed concerns that his child sometimes mixes up words between the two languages. Which of the following would be the best response for the teacher to provide the grandfather?

   A. document instances of the child mixing words to see if patterns exist
   B. inform the grandfather that this will continue for many years to come
   C. inform grandfather that this is common for the child's age
   D. conduct a formal assessment for placement of special education services

Answer: C

Explanation: Young children exposed to two languages at an early age typically mix up words between the two languages. The best approach is to inform the grandfather of this information to alleviate his concerns.

QUESTION 117

Before assigning a new chapter in the textbook, a special education social studies teacher walks students through the chapter's headings and subheadings. Prior to reading the entire chapter, the teacher encourages the students to read the chapter's introduction and summary. In taking this approach, the teacher is increasing comprehension of a content-area text by helping the students

- A. establish background knowledge of the topic.
- B. determine what is most critical to take away from the reading.
- C. increase awareness of entire chapter.
- D. analyze multiple viewpoints and perspectives.

Answer: B

Explanation: The introduction and summary contains the main information being communicated in the chapter. Having the student read the introduction and the summary, the teacher is helping the student in determining the most critical information to pay attention and take away from the reading.

QUESTION 118

What is the best question to ask about geography reasoning in second grade when walking through a street with houses, and then ending up on a street with several businesses?

    A. How long will it take to get back to the original destination?
    B. Why are houses and businesses located on different streets?
    C. Why do businesses have larger spaces than homes?
    D. Why are there more businesses than houses?

Answer: B

Explanation: As indicated in the question, the houses are on one street while the businesses are on a different street. The best question to understand is the reasoning for why houses and businesses are located on different streets.

QUESTION 119

Mr. Raymond has seen that John, who is claustrophobic and diagnosed with ADHD, has been the last person to turn in-class assignment 12 times in a row. His grades on the assignments are above average. What is the likely reason for John being the last person to turn in assignments?

    A. He double checks his work.
    B. He is shy to come up to the front.
    C. He does not want to come upfront while everyone is turning assignments.
    D. He is afraid someone might push him.

Answer: C

Explanation: John is claustrophobic, so going into crowded areas will be difficult for him. He is not going to want to come upfront while everyone is turning in assignments.

QUESTION 120

A teacher verbally directs a six-year-old student to perform a series of four sequential activities, and, then she obverse the student's performance. This approach is best for detecting which of the following?

- A. behavioral issues
- B. auditory memory issues
- C. cognitive impairment
- D. motor skill issues

Answer: B

Explanation: The student is asked to complete tasks in sequence, which requires the student to remember the information communicated verbally.

QUESTION 121

A special education teacher is ignoring a student's IEP recommendation. In fact, the teacher has not even looked at the student's IEP. This is:

- A. illegal
- B. legal
- C. professionally wrong
- D. acceptable as long as the student is learning

Answer: C

Explanation: The teacher's actions of not looking at the IEP are professionally wrong. The IEP is developed to support students in learning and differentiate lessons to tailor to students' needs.

QUESTION 122

For the last two weeks, a teacher has been abruptly ending lessons as she is unable to finish teaching. The best approach is to:

　　A. decrease the length of the lesson activity to complete on time
　　B. increase the speed of teaching
　　C. have students ask questions at the very end
　　D. find a way to end the lessons in a smooth manner even if the lesson is not completed

Answer: D

Explanation: Lessons can go over the allotted time. Teachers should not abruptly end the lesson as it can have a negative impact. The best option is to end the lesson in a smooth manner.

QUESTION 123

What kind of classroom instruction would a new teacher have to provide a student with Down syndrome?

　　A. involve the student in free activities
　　B. establish a more routine schedule
　　C. give direct instruction
　　D. provide individual instruction

Answer: C

Explanation: Direct instruction is the best option because the student will know exactly the expectations.

QUESTION 124

A special education, kindergarten, English Learner student spells the word found as "fawned". This is an example of:

A. self-generated words
B. pseudo-letter
C. pseudo-words
D. pseudo-sentence

Answer: A

Explanation: The student is making up words, so this is considered self-generated.

QUESTION 125

Which of the following is the best listening comprehension content for English Learners who have mastered basic structural forms but not vocabulary development?

A. vocabulary words to memorize
B. oral readings with accompanying pictures
C. television shows
D. flashcards

Answer: B

Explanation: The question asks for listening skills, so A and D is eliminated. Television shows are not the best way to develop vocabulary words, so C is eliminated. The best way is to do oral reading and have pictures to help understand vocabulary words.

ILTS Learning Behavior Specialist I (155)

Illinois Licensure Testing System

CPSIA information can be obtained
at www.ICGtesting.com
Printed in the USA
LVOW09s1101160517
534713LV00016B/417/P